The
Kite Runner

(PLAY SCRIPT)

The
Kite Runner

(PLAY SCRIPT)

ADAPTED BY **MATTHEW SPANGLER**

BASED ON THE NOVEL BY **KHALED HOSSEINI**

RIVERHEAD BOOKS

NEW YORK

2018

RIVERHEAD BOOKS
An imprint of Penguin Random House
375 Hudson Street
New York, New York 10014

Library of Congress Cataloging-in-Publication Data
Names: Spangler, Matthew J., author. | Hosseini, Khaled. Kite runner.
Title: The kite runner: based on the novel by Khaled Hosseini / adapted by Matthew Spangler.
Description: New York: Riverhead Books, 2018.
Identifiers: LCCN 2017027235 (print) | LCCN 2017032641 (ebook) |
ISBN 9780525534464 (ebook) | ISBN 9780735218062 (softcover)
Subjects: LCSH: Hosseini, Khaled. Kite runner—Adaptations. |
Kabul (Afghanistan)—Drama. | Male friendship—Drama. | Social classes—Drama. |
Betrayal—Drama. | Boys—Drama. | GSAFD: Bildungsromans.
Classification: LCC PS3619.P3424 (ebook) |
LCC PS3619.P3424 K58 2018 (print) | DDC 812/.6—dc23
LC record available at https://lccn.loc.gov/2017027235
p.   cm.

Printed in the United States of America
1   3   5   7   9   10   8   6   4   2

Book design by Gretchen Achilles

THE KITE RUNNER

KHALED HOSSEINI was born in Kabul, Afghanistan, and moved to the United States in 1980. He is the author of the *New York Times* bestsellers *The Kite Runner*, *A Thousand Splendid Suns*, and *And the Mountains Echoed*. He is a U.S. Goodwill Envoy to the United Nations Refugee Agency and the founder of the Khaled Hosseini Foundation, a nonprofit that provides humanitarian assistance to the people of Afghanistan.

MATTHEW SPANGLER is a playwright, director, and professor of performance studies at San José State University in California. His adaptation of *The Kite Runner* received five San Francisco Bay Area Theatre Critics Circle Awards, including Best Original Script and Best Overall Production. It has subsequently been produced by theaters throughout the United States, Canada, and the United Kingdom, including Wyndham's Theatre and the Playhouse Theatre on London's West End. Some of his other plays include *Tortilla Curtain*, adapted from the novel by T. C. Boyle; *Albatross*, based on Samuel Taylor Coleridge's poem "The Rime of the Ancient Mariner"; *A Paradise It Seems*, based on John Cheever's short stories; *Together Tea*, adapted from the novel by Marjan Kamali; *Masquerade*, from Jasmin Darznik's short story; adaptations of James Joyce's *Dubliners* and *Finnegans Wake*; as well as adaptations of John Steinbeck's and Ernest Hemingway's fiction. His book, *Staging Intercultural Ireland: New Plays and Practitioner Perspectives* (Cork University Press), coedited with Charlotte McIvor, explores the intersection of migration and the performing arts in Ireland.

The
Kite Runner

(PLAY SCRIPT)

This stage adaptation of *The Kite Runner* received its world premiere at the San Jose Repertory Theater, California, on March 21, 2009, with the following cast and creative team:

Amir	Barzin Akhavan
Rahim Khan/Zaman	Gregor Paslawsky
Young Amir	Craig Piaget
Sohrab Hassan	Lowell Abellon
Ali/Omar Faisal	James Saba
Baba	Thomas Fiscella
Assef	Adam Yazbeck
General Taheri/Farid	Demosthenes Chrysan
Soraya/Mrs. Nguyen	Rinabeth Apostol
Wali/Ensemble	Zarif Kabier Sadiqi
Kamal/Ensemble	Wahab Shayek
Ensemble	Lani Carissa Wong
Tabla player	Salar Nader
Director	David Ira Goldstein
Composer	Salar Nader
Set designer	Vicki Smith
Costume designer	Kish Finnegan
Lighting and projection designer	David Lee Cuthbert
Sound designer	Scott Edwards
Cultural consultant	Humaira Ghilzai

An early version of *The Kite Runner* was produced at San José State University in February 2007.

The production at Wyndham's Theatre, London, was produced by Martin Dodd for UK Productions Ltd, and Derek Nicol and Paul Walden for Flying Entertainment; it was originally a coproduction between Nottingham Playhouse and Liverpool Everyman & Playhouse. It ran in the West End from December 21, 2016, with the following cast and creative team:

Amir .... Ben Turner

Baba .... Emilio Doorgasingh

Rahim Khan .... Nicholas Khan

Soraya .... Lisa Zahra

Kamal .... David Ahmad

Ali .... Ezra Faroque Khan

Assef .... Nicholas Karimi

General Taheri .... Antony Bunsee

Tabla player .... Hanif Khan

Wali .... Bhavin Bhatt

Hassan/Sohrab .... Andrei Costin

Ensemble/Cover .... Johndeep More

Ensemble/Cover .... Natasha Karp

Director .... Giles Croft

Designer .... Barney George

Lighting designer .... Charles Balfour

Projection designer .... William Simpson

Composer/Musical director .... Jonathan Girling

Sound designer .... Drew Baumohl

Cultural consultant .... Humaira Ghilzai

Production director .... Andy Batty

Movement director .... Kitty Winter

Fight director .... Philip d'Orléans

Accent coach .... Sally Hague

Staff director .... Julia Locascio

Assistant director .... Allie Spencer

Casting directors .... Lucy Jenkins CDG and
Sooki McShane CDG

CHARACTERS (IN ORDER OF APPEARANCE)

Amir

Rahim Khan, *Baba's business partner*

Hassan, *Amir's childhood servant and best friend*

Ali, *Hassan's father and Baba's servant*

Baba, *Amir's father*

Assef, *neighborhood bully*

Radio Announcer, *voice-over*

Wali, *Assef's friend*

Kamal, *Assef's friend*

Kite Runners and Flyers, *ensemble*

Woman

Merchant

Birthday Party Guests, *ensemble*

Afghan Refugees, *ensemble*

Husband

Wife

Two Russian Soldiers, *the second more senior than the first*

1980s Americans, *ensemble*

Kid on Skateboard, *a member of ensemble*

Mrs. Nguyen, *Vietnamese shop owner*

General Taheri, *Soraya's father*

Soraya, *Amir's wife*

Dr. Schneider, *American oncologist*

Two Taliban Officials

Farid, *driver*

Zaman, *orphanage director*

Two Taliban Guards

Sohrab, *Hassan's son*

Omar Faisal, *Pakistani/American immigration attorney*

Raymond Andrews, *American embassy official in Pakistan*

Pakistani Doctor, *surgeon in a hospital in Pakistan*

A NOTE ON AMIR AND THE ENSEMBLE

Although Amir is onstage for the entire performance, this is an ensemble piece. The ensemble should be used as much as possible to fill the stage with movement in necessary scenes and to embody many of the descriptive passages. The kite tournament, in particular, should feature the entire cast. Amir should be physically active during his monologues, interacting with other characters and reliving what he describes with the emotional energy of the present, as if experiencing these events for the first time.

SUGGESTED DIVISION OF ROLES

Actor #1 .... *Amir*

Actor #2 .... *Baba, Taliban Guard*

Actor #3 .... *Hassan, Sohrab, Ensemble*

Actor #4 .... *Assef, Kid on Skateboard, Ensemble*

Actor #5 .... *Ali, Husband, Taliban Official, Taliban Guard, Omar Faisal, Ensemble*

Actor #6 .... *Rahim Khan, Russian Soldier #2, Dr. Schneider, Pakistani Doctor, Ensemble*

Actor #7 ....*General Taheri, Merchant, Russian Soldier #1, Raymond Andrews, Ensemble*

Actor #8 .... *Wali, Radio Announcer, Talib Official, Ensemble, and Farid or Omar Faisal*

Actor #9 ....*Kamal, Ensemble, and Farid or Omar Faisal*

Actress #1 .... *Soraya, Ensemble*

Actress #2 .... *Mrs. Nguyen, Woman, Wife*

If needed, the same actress could play both Actress #1 *and* Actress #2. *There is also a version of the script in which two actors play* Amir *in Act One: a younger* Amir *and an older/storyteller* Amir. *This version of the* script has been used for the U.S. and Canadian productions of the play. If you would be interested in viewing this script—with an older and younger Amir *in Act One*—please contact the playwright or his agent.

A NOTE ON MUSIC AND RECORDED SOUND

Music and sound-effect cues should figure prominently in the performance. Many productions have used a live tabla player onstage throughout Act One and the second half of Act Two. Whether the production has a live musician or not, music should be used widely in the transitions between scenes and to underscore moments within scenes. Sound-effect cues should also be used to help identify changes in location.

Act One

SCENE ONE

San Francisco, California, 2001. Tabla music. A bare stage, except for a blue-sky backdrop, marked by some clouds. The Ensemble stands facing the audience. Amir is center stage. Music fades out.

AMIR: I became what I am today at the age of twelve. I remember the precise moment, crouching behind a mud wall on a frigid winter day in 1975 . . . looking into a deserted alley. It's wrong what they say about the past, about how you can bury it, because the past claws its way out.

Beat.

Last summer, I got a phone call from Rahim Khan.

RAHIM KHAN: Come see me. There is a way to be good again.

AMIR: He had been my father's friend and business partner when we lived in Afghanistan.

RAHIM KHAN: Please. Come see me.

AMIR: Afterward, I went for a long walk in Golden Gate Park. I saw a pair of kites looking down on San Francisco, the city I now call home.

Gesturing to each in turn.

I thought about Baba, Rahim Khan, Ali, and most of all, Hassan, the best kite runner in Kabul and my best friend.

Beat.

I thought about how the winter of 1975 changed everything.

SCENE TWO

Kabul, Afghanistan, 1973. Fast-paced tabla music. Everyone exits, except Amir and Hassan, who break into a run. Amir holds two American Western-style revolvers and is firing them at Hassan as he chases him around the stage. Hassan occasionally fires back with his slingshot.

The boys are playing cowboys and Indians with Amir as the cowboy and Hassan as the Indian.

As they run, they yell lines like "I got you!," "No, you didn't!," "Got you that time!," "No you didn't!" Ad lib. These lines and the lines below could be done in either Dari or English. If Dari: "Ma giriftem et!" ["I got you!"], "Nay, na gerefteem!" ["No, you didn't!"], "Oo dafa gerifitem et!" ["Got you that time!"], "Inja pas biya!" ["Come back here!"].

After they run around the stage a bit, they face each other, head-on, as in a Western-style duel.

AMIR: Ba een shar baray hardo ma jay naste! [*This town ain't big enough for the two of us!*]

Hassan charges directly at Amir, but Amir manages to trip him and Hassan stumbles and falls. Amir stands over him and unloads his weapon on Hassan, shot after shot. Hassan laughs and protects himself from the invisible bullets.

HASSAN: Kho, kho, girifteem, girifteem! Bas ast! Ma goftom ke girifteem! [*Okay, okay, you got me, you got me! Stop! I said you got me!*]

Beat.

Ey, bebeen, ma chee darom. [*Hey, look what I got.*]

Hassan reaches into his pocket and pulls out a small mirror.

AMIR: To awordeesh! [*You brought it!*]

HASSAN: Beya, borame sar e darakht bala shawame! [*Come on, let's go climb the tree!*]

AMIR: Ma paysh as too mayrasom! [*Beat you to the top!*]

They climb high into a tree and, sitting on a branch, attempt to reflect the stage lights off the mirror into the eyes of the audience.

When we were kids growing up in Kabul, Hassan and I used to climb the poplar trees in the driveway of my father's estate. We'd annoy our neighbors by reflecting sunlight into their homes with a mirror. Sometimes I'd talk Hassan into firing walnuts with his slingshot at the neighbor's one-eyed German shepherd.

HASSAN: Ma na maykhayom. [*I don't want to.*]

AMIR: Beya, sat e ma tare maysha. [*Come on, it'll be fun.*]

HASSAN: Nay. [*No.*]

AMIR: Lutfan. Yak dafa. [*Please. Just one.*]

HASSAN: Ma goftom nay. [*I said no.*]

AMIR: Hassan, bar e ma bokoo. [*Then do it for me, Hassan.*]

Hassan hesitates.

Yad et basha ke nokar kee hastee. [*Remember whose servant you are.*]

HASSAN: Kho, ama tana baray to maykonom. [*Well, okay. But only for you.*]

Hassan takes out his slingshot and points it in the direction of the audience. Hassan is about to shoot the dog when Ali enters. He's doing laundry and carries a sheet over his arm.

ALI: Hassan, da o bala chee maykonee?! Az darakht payeen show! [*Hassan, what are you doing up there?! Come down from that tree!*]

HASSAN: Bobakhshee, Padar. [*Sorry, Father.*]

AMIR: (*as the boys descend from the tree*) Hassan's father, Ali, was my father's servant. They'd been together for over forty years.

ALI: Shaytan ayna ra roshanee mayta wa roshanee esh musilmana ra az namaz mindaza. Wa ba ayn e zaman khanda moykonad. Biya, ma ra komak ko ba rakht shoyee. [*The devil shines mirrors, too, shines them to distract Muslims during prayer. And he laughs while he does it. Now, come into the house and help me with this laundry.*]

HASSAN: Kho, Padar. [*Yes, Father.*]

AMIR: Ali, majbor ast ke bora? Namataname ke dega bazee koname? Padar hatman ejaza meyta. [*Does he have to, Ali? Can't we play just a little while longer? I'm sure Father wouldn't mind.*]

ALI: Kho, bad az ee ke bazee khlas shood. Ama yak daqeeqa zeyad tar nay! [*Okay, when you're done playing. But not one moment after!*]

AMIR: Ali, tashakor. [*Thanks, Ali.*]

Ali exits.

AMIR: (*touching Hassan as in tag*) You're it!

Hassan chases Amir around the stage and eventually tags him.

Amir then chases Hassan, who exits. Amir remains on stage.

I spent my entire childhood playing with Hassan on the grounds of my father's estate. My Baba was one of the richest merchants in all of Kabul, and everyone agreed he had built the most beautiful house in the Wazir Akbar Khan, the city's most affluent neighborhood. A redbrick driveway flanked by rosebushes led to a house of marble floors and wide windows. Gold-stitched tapestries lined the walls and crystal chandeliers hung from the ceiling. A terrace overlooked a garden and rows of cherry trees. And on the edge of the garden was the servants' shack, where Hassan and his father lived.

Hassan returns to the stage and faces out, as if frozen in memory. Amir might approach Hassan here, as if reaching out to the memory.

Every day when we were done playing, I would go to Baba's mansion, Hassan would go to his mud shack. It was there that Hassan was born, just one year after my mother died giving birth to me. Hassan's mother suffered a fate most Afghans consider far worse than death: she ran off with a troupe of musicians and actors. So my Baba hired the same woman who had nursed me to nurse Hassan. We took our first steps on the same lawn. And under the same roof, we spoke our first words. Mine was *Baba*. His was—

HASSAN: (*to Amir*) Amir!

AMIR: My name.

Hassan breaks the pose and they play tag again.

HASSAN: (*tagging Amir*) You're it!

AMIR: (*as he runs*) Hassan and I would play tag, hide-and-seek, cowboys and Indians. We spent entire winters flying kites. And we saw our first Western together—*Rio Bravo* with John Wayne.

Gunshots and music from Rio Bravo.

SCENE THREE

Baba's study. The music fades as Baba and Ali enter. Baba is smoking a pipe. Ali carries a hatbox. Ali removes the top of the box and takes out a brand-new leather cowboy hat, which he presents to Baba. Baba puts his pipe down and looks over the hat, checking for imperfections.

HASSAN: Ask him, Agha. Go on, ask him.

AMIR: Okay, okay, I will. Baba, can I come in?

BABA: No. This is grown-ups' time.

AMIR: But Hassan and I were wondering something.

BABA: (*quickly putting the cowboy hat back in the box*) What do you want, Amir?

AMIR: (*entering Baba's study*) Will you take us to Iran to meet John Wayne? Please.

BABA: What?

AMIR: We want to go to Iran to meet John Wayne. He lives there. So will you take us?

BABA: What makes you think John Wayne lives in Iran?

AMIR: He's in all the movies we see at the Iranian cinema.

BABA: (*laughing*) John Wayne doesn't live in Iran. Is Hassan with you?

AMIR: No.

Baba turns and sees Hassan lingering outside the study.

BABA: Why, there he is. Come in here, Hassan. Come on.

Hassan enters the study and approaches Baba, who puts his arm around Hassan's shoulders.

BABA: Now, listen, and I'll tell you how these films are made.

AMIR: (*to us*) Then he explained the concept of voice dubbing.

BABA: So, you see, John Wayne doesn't speak Farsi, and he isn't Iranian. He's an American.

Baba laughs, pats Hassan on the head.

AMIR: (*to us*) We saw *Rio Bravo* three times and *The Magnificent Seven* with Charles Bronson thirteen times. Turned out, Charles Bronson wasn't Iranian either.

BABA: Hassan, I have something for you.

Baba takes the leather cowboy hat out of the box.

It's your birthday tomorrow, so I may as well give you this now.

He presents the hat to Hassan.

AMIR: (*to us*) He never missed Hassan's birthday.

HASSAN: Wow!

BABA: Just like the one Clint Eastwood wore in *The Good, the Bad, and the Ugly.*

HASSAN: (*impressed*) Thank you, Agha sahib.

Hassan puts the hat on his head, but he puts it on backward, and it doesn't fit right. Baba laughs and turns the hat around, straightening it.

BABA: Happy birthday, Hassan.

Baba hugs Hassan.

Now, run along, boys.

Music from The Magnificent Seven *as Baba and Ali exit. As soon as they are a safe distance away, Amir steals the hat from Hassan and puts it on his own head.*

HASSAN: Hey!

The boys run around the stage playing cowboys and Indians until the music fades.

SCENE FOUR

A street in Kabul.

AMIR: (*to us*) One day, we were walking home from the cinema when we saw Assef approaching.

Assef enters, comes downstage, and, facing the audience, strikes a menacing pose with a pair of brass knuckles. He punches the air several times. Amir and Hassan stop playing and watch him with apprehension.

AMIR: (*to us*) If you were a kid in our neighborhood, you knew about Assef and his brass knuckles, but hopefully not through personal experience.

ASSEF: (*turning to Amir and Hassan*) Why, look who it is, it's Flat-Nose and Faggot!

AMIR: What do you want, Assef?

ASSEF: I just want to talk, Faggot. That okay?

Amir shrugs.

ASSEF: You plan to be in the kite-fighting tournament this winter?

AMIR: Maybe.

ASSEF: And your flat-nosed Hazara here going to be your kite runner?

AMIR: Yeah.

ASSEF: Well, you better watch out, because *I* run all the best kites.
   They're mine, you hear?

Amir nods.

   Answer me when I ask you a question!

Assef shoves Amir.

ASSEF: You hear me?

AMIR: Yes, Assef.

ASSEF: You know why they call me "Assef the Ear Eater," don't you?
   I really did bite that kid's ear off. Too bad he lives in Kandahar
   or I'd introduce you, so you can see what I'm capable of. And I'll
   do the same to you—or worse, if you cross me. Got it?

AMIR: Yes.

ASSEF: Give me that!

Assef takes the cowboy hat from Amir and puts it on his head.

   How do I look, boys? Just like John Wayne, huh?

*Shooting imaginary guns at Amir and Hassan, a hint of the sociopath
later to come.*

   Bang! Bang! Bang! Bang! Bang! Bang! Bang! Bang! Bang!
   BANG!

*He continues at full volume and an increasing pace, until he is out of
breath.*

   (*laughing*) I just killed you both!

He blows the smoke from the ends of his imaginary guns.

HASSAN: (*turning to Assef*) Please leave us alone, Agha.

ASSEF: Ooh, "Please leave us alone" he says. (*To Amir.*) So, you let your Hazara stand up for you, is that it, Amir? (*To Hassan.*) Hey, you slant-eyed Hazara, I knew your mother, knew her real well. When I took her from behind, she said the same thing, "Please leave me alone, Agha." What a tight little sugary cunt she had.

Ali enters.

ALI: What's going on here, boys?

ASSEF: Why, I was just complimenting your son on what a beautiful family he comes from.

ALI: Amir, your father wants you home. Come on.

Amir moves quickly to join Ali. As Ali exits, Hassan remains onstage, holding his ground with Assef. Tension builds. Then Hassan snatches the cowboy hat from Assef's head, and, before Assef can react, Hassan runs to join Ali offstage. Assef makes a quick move. His impulse is to run after Hassan, but Ali's presence makes him stop short.

ASSEF: Yeah, you better run! Get out of here while you still can!

AMIR: Years later, I learned an English word for the creature that Assef was, a word for which there is no Farsi equivalent: *sociopath*.

ASSEF: (*exiting in the other direction*) See you around, Flat-Nose! You too, Faggot!

SCENE FIVE

AMIR: Assef wasn't the only one to call Hassan *Flat-Nose*. It was a common slur. My people, the Pashtuns, had persecuted the Hazaras in the nineteenth century. They drove the Hazaras from their land and burned their homes, mostly because Pashtuns are Sunni Muslims and Hazaras are Shi'a. I spent the first twelve years of my life playing with Hassan, but I never really thought of him as a friend. History and religion aren't easy to overcome. In the end, I was Pashtun, he was Hazara; I was Sunni, he was Shi'a. Nothing was ever going to change that. But we were kids who had learned to crawl together, and nothing was going to change that either.

Tabla music. Hassan enters at a run. Amir joins him. The hill behind Baba's mansion. Amir holds a book and a small pocketknife. They stop running at the base of a tree, and Amir begins carving in it with the knife.

AMIR: (*to us*) There was a pomegranate tree on the hill behind my father's property.

HASSAN: What does it say, Amir agha?

AMIR: It says, "Amir and Hassan, the Sultans of Kabul!"

HASSAN: That makes it official, then. This tree belongs to us!

Beat.

Did you bring the book?

AMIR: (*pulls out a leather-bound book*) Right here.

Amir and Hassan sit on the ground and start reading the book.

That Hassan would grow up illiterate like most Hazaras was decided the minute he was born. So I read him stories. My favorite part was when we came across a big word he didn't know.

HASSAN: Amir agha, what does that word mean?

AMIR: Which one?

HASSAN: "Im-be-cile."

AMIR: "Imbecile"? You don't know what that means?

HASSAN: No.

AMIR: But it's such a common word. Everyone knows what it means! Let's see: "Imbecile." It means . . . smart, intelligent. I'll use it in a sentence. When it comes to words, Hassan is an imbecile.

HASSAN: Aaah, I see. Thanks, Amir agha.

AMIR: You're welcome. (*To us.*) I'd always feel guilty about it later, but I told myself it was nothing but a harmless prank.

HASSAN: Go on, read the story, Agha.

AMIR: (*to us*) Hassan's favorite book was the *Shahnamah*, the tenth-century epic of ancient Persian heroes. And his favorite story was "Rostam and Sohrab." (*Acting out the story in pantomime.*) In the story, the great warrior Rostam mortally wounds his nemesis, Sohrab, only to discover that Sohrab is his long-lost son. With his dying breath, Sohrab looked up at Rostam and said, "Thou

art indeed my father, and thou hast stained thy sword in the life-
blood of thy son."

HASSAN: Read it again, Amir agha. Please, read it again.

AMIR: No more today. We should be getting home. Come on.

Hassan exits.

AMIR: (*to us*) Hassan loved that story. But, personally, I didn't see
the tragedy of Rostam's fate. Don't all fathers harbor a desire to
kill their sons?

SCENE SIX

Baba's study. Baba enters with a glass of scotch in his hand. He stands downstage, hard-faced, as if gazing out of a window.

AMIR: I always felt like my father hated me a little. He molded the world around him to his liking, with me as the glaring exception. Legend had it he had wrestled a black bear with nothing but his hands. And once, just to prove he could, he built an orphanage outside Kabul. Drew up the blueprints himself, funded the entire project.

Over the next line, Baba turns away and pours himself another glass of scotch.

But I remembered all the times he didn't come home until after dark, all the times I ate dinner alone. I remember hating the kids in that orphanage.

Amir watches Baba for a moment, as his father drinks from the glass.

AMIR: (*to us*) When I was in school, we had a mullah who told us that drinking was a sin. (*To Baba.*) Baba, does that make you a sinner?

BABA: Does what make me a sinner?

AMIR: Drinking alcohol.

BABA: You'll never learn anything from those bearded idiots.

AMIR: You mean the mullah?

BABA: I mean all of them. Piss on the beards of all those self-righteous monkeys. God help us if Afghanistan ever falls into their hands.

AMIR: But the mullah at school seems nice.

BABA: So did Genghis Khan. But you asked about sin. Okay, are you listening?

AMIR: Yes.

BABA: I'm going to talk to you man to man. Think you can handle that for once?

Amir nods.

Good. Now, there is only one sin, only one. And that is theft. Every other sin is a variation of theft. You understand?

AMIR: No.

BABA: When you kill a man, you steal a life. You steal his wife's right to a husband, rob his children of a father. When you tell a lie, you steal someone's right to the truth. When you cheat, you steal the right to fairness. You see?

AMIR: I think so.

BABA: There is no act more wretched than stealing. A man who takes what's not his to take, be it a life or a loaf of naan, I spit on such a man.

AMIR: Yes, Baba.

BABA: If there is a God out there, I hope he has more important things to attend to than my drinking scotch. Now, all this talk about sin has made me thirsty again.

Baba refills his glass.

AMIR: (*to us*) If Baba did hate me, why not? After all, I had killed his beloved wife. So the least I could've done was have the decency to turn out more like him. But I buried my head in books and wrote poetry.

BABA: Real men don't read poetry, and they certainly don't write it! Real men play soccer, just like your Baba did when he was young!

AMIR: (*to us*) He signed me up for soccer teams, but I was pathetic. Always offside or tripping over the ball and the harder I tried, the more I failed.

Rahim Khan enters, pen and notebook in hand, to discuss something business-related with Baba.

Then I wrote my first short story.

Amir cautiously approaches holding two sheets of paper.

AMIR: Baba?

BABA: What do you want, Amir?

AMIR: I wrote a story.

BABA: Good for you.

Long pause.

AMIR: Would you like to read it?

BABA: No. I mean, not now.

RAHIM KHAN: May I have it, Amir jan? I would very much like to read it.

BABA: Fine. Give it to Rahim Khan.

*Rahim Khan puts down the business notebook and takes Amir's short
story.*

RAHIM KHAN: (*reading from the story*) A man was walking in the
   mountains when he found a magic cup by the side of the path.
   He learned that if he cried into the cup, his tears would turn to
   pearls. But he was a happy man and rarely shed a tear, so—

BABA: That's enough. Maybe we can hear the rest later. Now, run
   along, Amir, and read your books. Rahim Khan and I are busy.

Amir doesn't move; Rahim Khan still has his story.

   I said run along.

AMIR: Yes, Baba.

*Amir leaves the study, but remains onstage, overhearing the following
conversation. Rahim Khan holds on to Amir's story.*

BABA: There's something about Amir that troubles me.

RAHIM KHAN: You should be grateful he's healthy.

BABA: I know, but he's always buried in those books or shuffling
   around like he's lost in some dream.

RAHIM KHAN: And?

BABA: And I wasn't like that.

RAHIM KHAN: Children aren't coloring books. You don't get to fill
   them with your favorite colors.

BABA: I'm telling you, I wasn't like that and neither were any of the
   kids I grew up with.

RAHIM KHAN: He's a pretty good kite fighter. A few times he's even
   come close to winning the tournament.

BABA: Coming close is not the same as winning. *I* didn't come close. I *won* the tournament when I was his age.

RAHIM KHAN: Sometimes you are the most self-centered man I know.

BABA: It has nothing to do with that.

RAHIM KHAN: Nay?

BABA: Nay.

RAHIM KHAN: Then what?

BABA: I see how the neighborhood boys push him around, take his toys, give him a shove here, a whack there. And he never fights back. Never. He just drops his head.

RAHIM KHAN: So he's not violent.

BABA: That's not what I mean. There's something *missing* in that boy. You know what happens when other boys tease him? Hassan steps in and fends them off.

RAHIM KHAN: Just let him find his way.

BABA: And where is he headed? A boy who won't stand up for himself becomes a man who can't stand up to anything.

RAHIM KHAN: You're just afraid he'll never take over the business from you.

BABA: Look, I know there's a fondness between you and him and I'm happy about that. He needs someone who understands him, because God knows I don't. It's like . . . if I hadn't seen the doctor pull him out of my wife with my own eyes, I'd never believe he was my son.

SCENE SEVEN

Sounds of explosions and gunfire. War breaks out. Rahim Khan exits, while the boys and their fathers run onto the stage and huddle together. Eventually, the sounds of explosions and gunfire fade out.

RADIO ANNOUNCER: King Zahir Shah's forty-year monarchy has come to an end. On this date, July 17, 1973, our new president, Daoud Khan, proudly proclaims Afghanistan a republic.

The danger seems to be over and Baba and Ali exit. Amir now holds a pencil and several sheets of paper in his hands. He is rewriting the short story about the man and the magic cup. Hassan sits next to him, pensive.

HASSAN: Amir agha, what's a "republic"?

AMIR: I don't know.

HASSAN: Amir agha?

AMIR: What?

HASSAN: Does "republic" mean Father and I will have to move away?

AMIR: I don't think so.

HASSAN: Amir agha?

AMIR: What?

HASSAN: I don't want them to send me and Father away.

AMIR: You donkey. No one's sending you away.

A pause.

HASSAN: Amir agha?

AMIR: *What!*

HASSAN: What are you doing?

AMIR: I'm working on a story I wrote.

HASSAN: A story? You mean, like "Rostam and Sohrab"?

AMIR: Well, yeah, kind of.

HASSAN: What's it about?

AMIR: (*proud of his story*) It's about a man who finds a magic cup, and every time he cries into the cup his tears turn into pearls. So he finds ways to make himself sad, and as the pearls pile up, he becomes greedier and greedier. The story ends with the man sitting on a mountain of pearls. He's holding a bloody knife and crying into the cup, and at his feet is his wife's dead body.

Hassan does not respond.

What do you think?

HASSAN: That's a sad story.

AMIR: But do you like it?

HASSAN: (*after a brief pause*) Yes, I do. . . . But will you permit me to ask a question?

AMIR: Of course.

HASSAN: Well, if I may ask, why does the man kill his wife? In fact, why does he ever have to feel sad to shed tears? Can't he just smell an onion?

Pause as Hassan's words sink in. The point had never occurred to Amir.
He is stunned and a little angry. He turns away and crumples up the
story.

Hey, you want to go up to the pomegranate tree?

AMIR: Yeah, all right, let's go.

HASSAN: (*tags Amir*) You're it!

They break into laughter as Amir chases Hassan.

SCENE EIGHT

The hill behind Baba's mansion. Assef, Wali, and Kamal enter.

Assef is tossing a rock in his hand.

ASSEF: Hey, lovers! Wait up!

Amir and Hassan stop running. They stand still, afraid of what Assef might do.

ASSEF: Have you heard the news, boys? The king is gone. Good riddance, I say.

WALI: Long live the president!

ASSEF: My father knows the president, did you know that, Amir?

AMIR: So does my father.

ASSEF: (*mimicking*) "So does my father."

Kamal and Wali laugh.

Well, he ate dinner at my house. How do you like that? You know what I'll tell him the next time he comes over? I'm going to have a little chat with him, man to man, tell him what your Hazara already knows: that Afghanistan is the land of Pashtuns. Always has been, always will be. We are the true Afghans, the pure Afghans, not this Flat-Nose here.

Assef shoves Hassan.

WALI: His people pollute our homeland!

KAMAL: They dirty our blood!

ASSEF: Afghanistan for Pashtuns, I say. I'm going to ask the president to rid our country of all the dirty Hazaras.

AMIR: Just let us go. We're not bothering you.

ASSEF: (*turning to face Amir*) Oh, you're bothering me, all right. You bother me very much. In fact, you bother me more than this Hazara. How can you talk to him, play with him, call him your "friend"?

AMIR: He's not my friend. He's my *servant!*

ASSEF: Yeah, well, *you're* the problem, Amir. If idiots like you and your father didn't take these people in, we'd be rid of them by now. You're a disgrace to Afghanistan.

Assef drops the rock and takes out his brass knuckles.

And I think it's time to teach you a little lesson.

Wali and Kamal grab Amir and pin his arms behind his back. As Assef gets ready to hit Amir, Hassan, without the others noticing, picks up the rock and inserts it into the cup of his slingshot. He pulls the sling back and points it at Assef's head. Just as Assef is about to punch Amir . . .

HASSAN: Leave us alone, Agha!

ASSEF: (*turning toward Hassan*) Put it down, you motherless Hazara.

HASSAN: Leave us be, Agha.

ASSEF: Maybe you didn't notice there are three of us and two of you.

HASSAN: Maybe *you* didn't notice that I'm the one holding the slingshot. If you make a move, they'll have to change your name from "Assef the Ear Eater" to "*One-Eyed* Assef."

ASSEF: (*pause, as he considers his odds*) You should know something about me, Flat-Nose: I'm a very patient person. This doesn't end today. And this isn't the end for you either, Amir. Someday, I'll make you face me one on one. (*To Wali and Kamal.*) Come on.

WALI: (*as they exit*) Your Hazara made a big mistake today, Amir.

KAMAL: A big mistake!

AMIR: (*to us*) Neither of us spoke as we walked home.

All exit except Amir.

SCENE NINE

The streets of Kabul. The music shifts to something fast-paced. The Ensemble enters and darts around the stage, as if chasing kites. One of them gives Amir a kite attached to a spool of glass-coated string. The music stops and the Ensemble freezes, gazing up at the sky, as if watching for falling kites.

AMIR: Winter used to be my favorite season in Kabul because it was the time of the kite-fighting tournament. Hassan and I built our own kites. We'd spend hours shaving bamboo for the center and cross spars, and cutting the tissue paper.

He hands the spool to a member of the Ensemble and then gives the kite to another Ensemble member. They stretch the string across the stage.

And then, we prepared our string—the glass-coated cutting line, the bullet in the chamber, ready to strike! We'd go out in the yard and feed five hundred feet of string through a mixture of ground glass and glue.

Amir runs his fingers along the string to show us how sharp it is.

The tournament started early in the morning and didn't end until the winning kite flew in the sky. The streets were filled with kite fighters, looking up, trying to gain position to cut an opponent's line. The lucky kite fighters had an assistant—in my case, Hassan—who held the spool and fed the string. But the real fun began when a kite was cut.

Amir snaps the string and suddenly the Ensemble comes to life and darts around the stage, yelling, as if chasing falling kites.

That was where the runners came in. They chased the falling kite through the streets until it came spiraling down. And the most coveted prize was the last fallen kite of the tournament. For this, fights broke out.

The Ensemble exits chasing the falling kites and yelling at one another with the energy of intense competition. Ad lib.

But Hassan was by far the greatest kite runner I'd ever seen.

SCENE TEN

Hassan enters in a run.

HASSAN: Amir! This way!

AMIR: No, Hassan! Wait! It's over there!

HASSAN: Come on!

AMIR: But you're going the wrong way!

Reluctantly, Amir joins Hassan in a run. Then Hassan stops running and waits, looking up at the sky. Amir stands beside him.

What are we doing here? Didn't you see the kite going that way?

HASSAN: It's coming.

AMIR: How do you know?

HASSAN: I know.

AMIR: But *how* do you know?

HASSAN: Would I ever lie to you, Amir agha?

AMIR: I don't know, would you?

HASSAN: I'd sooner eat dirt.

AMIR: Eat dirt? You'd do that?

HASSAN: (*his focus still on the sky*) Do what?

AMIR: Eat dirt if I told you to.

HASSAN: (*pause as he looks at Amir*) If you asked, I would. But I wonder, would you ever ask me to do such a thing, Amir agha?

AMIR: Don't be stupid. You know I wouldn't.

HASSAN: I know. (*Looking up.*) Look, here it comes!

Hassan raises his arms as if to catch the slowly falling kite.

AMIR: (*to us, as the kite comes drifting down from the sky*) And may
God—if He exists—strike me blind if the kite didn't just drop
into his outstretched arms.

*Hassan and Amir cheer, and together they chant "Sultans of Kabul!" three
times as they run toward the wings in celebration. Hassan exits with the
kite. Amir remains onstage.*

SCENE ELEVEN

The streets of Kabul.

AMIR: In the winter of 1975, the night before the tournament, it snowed heavily. The next morning the streets were glistening white.

The Ensemble enters laughing, chasing one another and throwing snow-balls. Baba and Rahim Khan stand on a rooftop overlooking the scene.

Word had it this was going to be the biggest tournament in twenty-five years. I had never seen so many people on our street. Rooftops were jammed with spectators. And the smell of lamb kabob drifted from open doors.

Hassan enters with their kite and prepares it for flying. The Ensemble also prepares for the kite tournament.

I looked up and saw Baba and Rahim Khan.

Amir waves. Baba nods back.

In order to win Baba's affection, I had to win this tournament. I wasn't going to fail him. Not this time.

HASSAN: Are you ready, Amir agha?

AMIR: Yeah, I'm ready.

HASSAN: Okay, let's fly!

Over the next line, Hassan runs across the stage, lifts the kite high above his head and tosses it in the air. This can be done entirely through mime or with an actual kite.

AMIR: Hassan ran and tossed the kite. Then it was rocketing toward
    the sky!

Fast-paced tabla music. Hassan runs back and Amir hands him the spool. The Ensemble members also fly kites. The kite flying could be done either through mime and choreographed movement or by using actual kites and/ or string. Amir should play the following scene with the immediate energy of the moment.

At least two dozen kites were already up there. Within an hour
the number doubled. Red, blue, and yellow kites glided and spun
past each other. And soon, the cutting started!

A kite is cut.

ENSEMBLE: *Cheering!*

In addition to cheering and clapping, the Ensemble might also say things like "Shahbash!" ["Bravo!"], "Aafarin!" ["Good job!"], "Waa waa!" ["Wow!"], and "Namekhoda!" ["God bless!"]. After an Ensemble member has his kite cut, he becomes a runner and darts across the stage trying to guess the position of where the kite will fall. The chase might take him offstage or even into the house. Eventually, each Ensemble member returns to watch the tournament play out. The kite tournament should build to an intense explosion of energy.

AMIR: And the first of the losing kites whirled out of control.

Another kite is cut by a member of the Ensemble.

ENSEMBLE: *Cheering and clapping!*

AMIR: (*looking in Baba's direction*) I glanced over at Baba. Was he pulling for me, or did he enjoy watching me fail?

HASSAN: Look out, Amir! Look out!

Amir quickly looks back at the sky.

AMIR: A red kite was closing in on mine! I tangled with it a bit, then cut him when he became impatient!

Amir pulls back hard on the string and cuts the kite.

ENSEMBLE: *Cheering!*

BABA: Shahbash! [*Bravo!*]

HASSAN: Nice job, Amir agha!

ENSEMBLE: *Continues cheering!*

BABA: Eyes on the sky, Amir!

HASSAN: Look out for that one!

AMIR: (*to Hassan*) I got him! (*To us.*) I sliced a bright yellow kite!

Amir cuts the kite.

ENSEMBLE: *Cheering!*

AMIR: And then one with a white tail!

Amir cuts the next one.

ENSEMBLE: *More cheering, louder and more intense.*

AMIR: My hands were bloody, but I didn't care! Eventually, the number of kites dwindled from fifty to a dozen. And I was one of them. I made it to the last dozen! (*To Hassan.*) This part of the tournament takes a while.

HASSAN: Yeah, guys who last this long are good.

BABA: (*to Amir*) They won't fall for simple tricks!

Another kite is cut, this time by a member of the Ensemble.

ENSEMBLE: *Cheering!*

AMIR: By three o'clock that afternoon, we were down to a half dozen.

HASSAN: Don't take your eyes off the sky.

AMIR: My legs ached and my neck was stiff. But with each defeated kite . . .

Amir cuts another kite.

ENSEMBLE: *Cheering!*

AMIR: Hope grew in my heart, like snow collecting on a wall, one flake at a time.

ENSEMBLE: *Cheering!*

HASSAN: Watch out for that blue one. He's cut a lot of kites.

AMIR: How many?

HASSAN: At least eleven in the last hour. Here he comes!

AMIR: (*to Hassan*) I see it! (*To us.*) The blue kite sliced a big purple one!

ENSEMBLE: *A loud cheer!*

AMIR: He swept the sky in a series of loops and cut three more!

ENSEMBLE: *Three distinct cheers as the three kites are cut. Each cheer grows in intensity from the previous one. The blue kite is impressive.*

AMIR: And suddenly it was just me and the blue kite! This was my one chance to cut loose my pain. I smelled victory! Salvation! Redemption!

ENSEMBLE: *Cheering loudly (ad lib). Clapping, whistling, stomping feet. The tension should build to a crescendo on Amir's line "And then!"*

HASSAN: Concentrate, Agha! Play it smart. . . .

BABA: Hang in there, Amir!

HASSAN: Be patient. . . .

A SINGLE MEMBER OF THE ENSEMBLE: *A loud whistle.*

ENSEMBLE: *(clapping, stomping feet, with growing intensity)* Boboresh! Boboresh! Boboresh! Boboresh! [*Cut him! Cut him!*]

A SINGLE MEMBER OF THE ENSEMBLE: Cut hiiiiim!

HASSAN: Almost there . . .

BABA: Don't force it, Amir!

AMIR: A gust of wind lifted my kite!

HASSAN: Now! Get on top!

BABA: Up, Amir, up!

AMIR: I pulled up! Looped my kite on top of the blue one!

HASSAN: You've got him!

AMIR: He was in trouble!

HASSAN: Cut him, Amir! Cut him!

BABA: Boboresh!

AMIR: I closed my eyes and loosened my grip!

HASSAN: That's it!

ENSEMBLE: *Cheering with intensity building to a climax.*

AMIR: The string sliced my fingers! And then . . .

Amir pulls down hard on his string!

A BEAT OF TOTAL SILENCE AS EVERYONE LOOKS UP AT THE SKY.

ENSEMBLE: *Motionless, silent, holding its breath. Then . . .*

HASSAN: BRAVO!

ENSEMBLE: *Loud cheering!*

Everyone erupts in cheers, clapping, laughing, and stomping their feet. The Ensemble continues to clap and cheer over the following lines.

HASSAN: Bravo, Amir agha! You did it!

AMIR: (*to us*) The blue kite was falling from the sky, spinning out of control!

The following lines should overlap.

HASSAN: You won, Amir agha! You won!

AMIR: I won, Hassan, I won!

BABA: You won, Amir! (*To us.*) That's my son, he won!

HASSAN: (*as the culminating line in the sequence of cheers*) YOU WON!

AMIR: No, *we* won, Hassan. *We* won!

HASSAN: I'm going to run that blue kite for you.

AMIR: Come back with it.

Pause, then with significance.

HASSAN: For you . . . a thousand times over.

Hassan exits, running after the kite. The Ensemble enthusiastically con-

gratulates Amir by patting his back and tousling his hair. Maybe they even lift him up on their shoulders and cheer. Then they exit in a run.

AMIR: Then I went to look for Hassan. I ran up and down every street.

Amir runs. A Woman enters, coming home from the market.

WOMAN: Amir jan, I heard you won the kite tournament. Congratulations!

AMIR: Have you seen Hassan?

WOMAN: Your servant?

AMIR: Yes.

WOMAN: I hear he's a great kite runner.

AMIR: He is. But have you seen him?

WOMAN: I think I saw him running toward the bazaar a while ago.

AMIR: Thanks!

Amir runs off and the Woman exits. A Merchant enters carrying a basket of bright red pomegranates.

AMIR: (*to the Merchant*) Agha?

MERCHANT: (*gruffly*) What?

AMIR: I'm looking for a Hazara, a kid about my age.

MERCHANT: What are you doing in the bazaar at this time of day looking for a Hazara?

AMIR: I need to find him.

MERCHANT: What's he to you?

AMIR: He's our servant's son.

MERCHANT: Lucky Hazara, having such a concerned master. His father should get on his knees, sweep the dust at your feet with his eyelashes.

AMIR: Are you going to tell me or not?

MERCHANT: I think I saw the boy you described running that way. He was carrying a blue kite.

AMIR: Yes!

MERCHANT: Of course, they've probably caught him by now.

AMIR: Who?

MERCHANT: The other boys, the ones chasing him. Boro! [*Get lost!*]

Amir runs away before the Merchant finishes speaking. The Merchant exits in the other direction. A loud whistle offstage.

WALI: (*offstage*) Over there!

KAMAL: (*getting closer*) Flat-Nose!

Hassan enters in a run, carrying a blue kite. Kamal enters from the wing Hassan is running toward, blocking his path. Hassan doubles back, but Wali enters from the wing Hassan just entered from. Then Assef enters upstage, rattling his brass knuckles. The stage is now the closed end of an alley, with Amir watching from the side. Assef, Wali, and Kamal close in on Hassan.

ASSEF: Where's your slingshot, Hazara? What was it you said? "They'll have to call me One-Eyed Assef." (*Turning to Wali and Kamal.*) Is that what he said?

WALI: That's what he said. "One-Eyed Assef."

ASSEF: Yes, that was clever.

KAMAL: Really clever!

ASSEF: Then again, it's easy to be clever when you're holding a loaded weapon. But today is your lucky day, because I'm in a mood to forgive. What do you say to that, boys?

KAMAL: That's generous.

WALI: Especially, after the rude manners he showed us last time.

ASSEF: Of course, nothing's free in this world, and my pardon comes with a small price: it's only going to cost you that blue kite. Fair deal, isn't it, boys?

WALI: More than fair.

KAMAL: After all, nothing's free.

HASSAN: Amir agha won the tournament, and I ran this kite for him. This is his kite.

ASSEF: A loyal Hazara. Loyal as a *dog*! But before you sacrifice yourself for him, think about this: Would he do the same for you? To him, you're nothing but an ugly pet. Don't fool yourself and think you're something more.

HASSAN: Amir agha and I are friends.

ASSEF: (*laughing*) Oh, "friends"? (*Turning to Wali and Kamal.*) You hear that? He says they're friends?

KAMAL: (*more laughter*) Friends!

WALI: That's a good one!

ASSEF: Someday you'll wake up from your little fantasy and learn how good a friend he really is. (*No longer laughing.*) Now, give us that kite! Last chance, Hazara.

HASSAN: No.

Assef thinks for a moment.

ASSEF: Okay, you know what? I've changed my mind. I'll let you keep the kite. So it'll always remind you of what I'm about to do.

Hassan gently sets the kite down and readies himself to fight. Assef, Wali, and Kamal rush Hassan and they struggle. Hassan puts up a good fight, but at last, he is pinned to the ground by Wali and Kamal. Assef loosens the top of his jeans.

So what do you say, boys?

WALI: I don't know, Assef. My father says it's sinful.

ASSEF: Your father won't find out! And there's nothing sinful about teaching a lesson to a disrespectful donkey.

WALI: I don't know.

ASSEF: Suit yourself. What about you?

KAMAL: I . . . ah, well . . .

ASSEF: It's just a Hazara!

KAMAL: I don't think I can.

ASSEF: Fine. All I want you weaklings to do is hold him down. Think you can manage that?

Wali and Kamal nod.

Come on, bring him over here.

Assef leads the exit, followed by Wali and Kamal dragging Hassan offstage. Amir describes the scene while facing the audience.

AMIR: Hassan's pants were pulled off. Assef unzipped his jeans, dropped his underwear, and knelt down. He grabbed Hassan by the hips. Hassan didn't struggle. Didn't even whimper. And I knew I had one last chance to decide who I was going to be. I could step into that alley, stand up for Hassan, and accept whatever would happen to me. Or, I could run. Then I saw tiny drops of blood fall from between Hassan's legs, stain the snow black . . . and I ran.

Fast-paced tabla music. Amir runs.

I ran as fast as I could. I ran all the way home.

Baba enters.

BABA: Congratulations, Amir!

Baba and Amir embrace. Amir buries his face in Baba's chest and cries.

You're a hero! There must have been a hundred kites up there. I knew you could do it! Shahbash! [*Bravo!*]

Hassan enters, picks up the blue kite, and walks toward Amir and Baba.

Congratulations to you, too, Hassan!

Amir turns and sees him. He leaves Baba's embrace and goes to Hassan.

AMIR: Where were you? I looked for you.

Hassan does not respond. They stand facing each other for a moment in silence. Then Hassan slowly holds out the kite. Amir looks at it. Will he take the kite or not? Then he extends his hands and slowly accepts the kite from Hassan. Baba walks over and puts his hand on Amir's shoulder.

BABA: Well done, Amir.

Baba and Amir walk to the other side of the stage with the kite, replaying the tournament. Hassan watches them for a moment, then exits in the other direction, alone.

SCENE TWELVE

Baba's mansion. Baba now holds the blue kite. He is looking at it admiringly.

AMIR: (*to us*) Maybe Hassan was the price I had to pay to win Baba. He was just a Hazara, wasn't he?

Beat.

Baba was proud for a few weeks and we immersed ourselves in the illusion that we saw each other in a way we never had. But soon things began to cool off.

Baba exits with the blue kite.

It didn't take long for him to resume going to his study and closing the door. As for Hassan, I could barely look at him, I was so crippled with guilt.

Ali enters with a rag in his hand. He's pretending to do some cleaning. He looks around to make sure no one is within earshot.

ALI: Amir.

AMIR: Yes, Ali.

ALI: Can I ask you something about Hassan?

AMIR: If you have to.

ALI: After the kite tournament, he came home bloodied and his shirt was torn. He said it was nothing, that he'd gotten into a scuffle with some boys over the kite.

AMIR: Yeah . . .?

ALI: Did something happen to him? Something he's not telling me?

AMIR: How should *I* know?

ALI: You would tell me if something happened, right?

AMIR: Like I said, how should I know!

ALI: Kho [*Okay*], but please tell me if you learn something.

AMIR: Yeah, I'll let you know.

Ali exits.

Hassan and I stopped playing together and I went out of my way to avoid him. But he continued to make my bed and iron my clothes. Everywhere I turned, I saw signs of his loyalty, his goddamn loyalty.

Hassan enters.

HASSAN: Amir agha.

AMIR: What?

HASSAN: I'm going to the baker to buy naan. I was wondering if . . . if you wanted to come along.

AMIR: I think I'm just going to stay here and read.

HASSAN: It's a sunny day.

AMIR: I can see that.

HASSAN: Might be fun to go for a walk.

AMIR: You go.

HASSAN: I wish you'd come.

AMIR: I don't want to.

HASSAN: Please tell me what I've done, Amir agha?

AMIR: You haven't done anything. Just go.

HASSAN: You can tell me. I'll stop doing it.

AMIR: I'll tell you what I want you to stop doing.

HASSAN: Anything.

AMIR: I want you to stop harassing me, that's what I want.

HASSAN: I'm sorry, Amir agha. But . . . why don't we play anymore?

AMIR: You want to play? Okay, what would you do if I hit you?

HASSAN: What?

AMIR: Hit you. Like this.

Amir hits Hassan in the face.

    What would you do?

He hits him again.

    Come on!

He hits him again.

    Hit me back! Hit me!

He continues hitting him until Hassan falls down.

    Get up! Hit me back! Hit me back, goddamn you! You're a coward, Hassan! Nothing but a goddamn coward!

Amir delivers one final blow to Hassan, a sharp kick to the stomach. Hassan slowly stands and faces Amir.

HASSAN: Do you feel better, Amir agha?

Hassan exits. Baba enters holding a large pair of garden shears.

BABA: I'm going to cut back the rose bushes, Amir. I could use some help.

AMIR: Baba, have you ever thought about getting new servants?

BABA: What did you say?

AMIR: I was just wondering, that's all.

BABA: Why would I get rid of Hassan and Ali?

AMIR: Just a question.

BABA: I grew up with Ali. Forty years he's been with my family. Forty goddamn years. And you think I'm just going to throw him out? As for Hassan . . . he's not going anywhere, you understand?

AMIR: Yes, Baba.

BABA: He's staying right here with us! This is Hassan's home and we're his family!

AMIR: I'm sorry.

BABA: I've never laid a hand on you, Amir, but you ever say that again . . . You bring me shame.

Baba exits.

SCENE THIRTEEN

Baba's mansion.

AMIR: But for my birthday that summer, Baba threw a party. Though he only did it because I won the kite tournament: he wanted to show me off.

Music. The Ensemble enters from as many points as possible singing, "Tawalod, tawalod, tawalod et mubarak, mubarak, mubarak, tawalod et mubarak" ["Happy Birthday"]. *At the end of the song, everyone claps for Amir. A large table, piled high with gifts and food, is brought onstage. Music plays. People turn to one another and dance and socialize. A party atmosphere. Ali approaches Amir and extends a book to him.*

ALI: Happy birthday, Amir. Hassan and I got this for you. It's the *Shahnamah* with colored illustrations.

Amir takes the book, though he knows he doesn't deserve it.

It's modest and not worthy of you, but we hope you like it.

AMIR: It's beautiful.

ALI: Hassan said your copy is old and ragged, and some of the pages are missing. All the pictures are hand-drawn in this one with pen and ink.

AMIR: Thank you, Ali. And thank Hassan for me.

ALI: I will. Tawalod et mubarak, Amir agha.

Ali moves away to serve the party guests. Assef steps forward with a shiny new soccer ball under his arm.

ASSEF: Happy birthday, Amir! Great party! Here, I know how you like to play soccer, so I got you a little gift. Hope you like it.

Assef holds out the soccer ball, but Amir does not take it.

BABA: (*coming over*) Well, Amir?

AMIR: What?

BABA: Aren't you going to thank Assef jan? That was very considerate of him.

AMIR: (*reluctantly accepting the soccer ball from Assef*) Thanks.

BABA: Still playing soccer, Assef jan?

ASSEF: Of course, Kaka jan.

Baba takes the ball from Amir to get a better look at it.

BABA: Right wing, as I recall?

ASSEF: Actually, I switched to center forward this year. You get to score more that way.

BABA: You know, I played center forward, too, when I was young.

Baba passes the soccer ball to Assef, bouncing it off his knee. Assef catches it with his hands.

ASSEF: I'll bet you still could if you wanted to.

Assef passes the ball back, also bouncing it off his knee.

BABA: Your flattering ways are becoming world famous.

ASSEF: We're thinking about playing a little game tomorrow at my house, Amir. Maybe you'll join us. Bring Hassan if you want to.

BABA: That sounds fun. What do you think, Amir?

AMIR: I don't want to go.

BABA: I'm sorry, Assef jan. I don't know what's wrong with him.

ASSEF: No harm done. You have an open invitation anyway. Happy birthday, Amir.

AMIR: Thanks for coming.

ASSEF: I wouldn't miss your party for anything. See you around.

Music. Baba and Assef dance side by side, as they return to the other party guests.

The Ensemble exits or turns upstage in the attitude of a soft freeze. Amir puts the book on the table and moves downstage. The music fades out.

Amir sits on the front edge of the stage. Rahim Khan enters, carrying a glass of scotch.

RAHIM KHAN: Shouldn't you be entertaining your guests?

AMIR: They don't need me for that. (*Noticing the glass in Rahim Khan's hand.*) I didn't know you drank.

RAHIM KHAN: Turns out I do. But only on the most important occasions.

Beat.

May I sit down?

AMIR: If you want.

Rahim Khan sits next to Amir and looks up at the night sky.

RAHIM KHAN: It's a beautiful evening.

AMIR: I guess.

RAHIM KHAN: (*pause*) Here. Happy birthday.

He reveals a fancy leather-bound notebook. He opens it and begins to read from Amir's story about the man and the magic cup, which he has placed inside.

"A man was walking in the mountains when he found a magic cup." For your stories. God has granted you a special talent. It is your duty to hone that talent, because a person who wastes his God-given talent is a donkey.

He gives the book to Amir.

AMIR: Thank you, Rahim Khan.

RAHIM KHAN: (*pause*) Did I ever tell you I almost got married once?

AMIR: You did?

RAHIM KHAN: It's true. I was eighteen. Her name was Mena, and she was the most beautiful girl I'd ever seen. She was from India. Her father owned a business importing silk, and they lived in the house next to ours. We used to meet secretly because we knew that neither of our families would approve. But we had this fantasy that one day we'd have a big fancy wedding and invite everyone, from Kabul to Calcutta. Well, eventually, I got up the courage to tell my father. You should have seen his face. My mother fainted. My brother went to fetch his hunting rifle before my father stopped him. And Mena's parents . . . I don't even want to tell you how they reacted at the prospect of their Hindu daughter marrying a Muslim. It was the two of us against the world.

AMIR: So what happened?

RAHIM KHAN: The world won. Her father sold his business and they moved back to India. And that was the last I saw of her.

AMIR: I'm sorry.

RAHIM KHAN: It was a long time ago. Zendagi migzara. Life goes on.

Beat.

My door is always open to you.

AMIR: Thanks.

Pause. They look at each other. Amir looks away. Then . . .

Do you remember the day of the kite tournament—

He stops himself.

RAHIM KHAN: Yes . . .

AMIR: Nothing. Thanks for the book.

Rahim Khan smiles. He knows Amir is holding something back, but he is not going to push the matter further. At that moment, loud explosions and sudden flashes of light fill the sky.

RAHIM KHAN: Look, your Baba got fireworks. Come on, we'd better get back.

Rahim Khan and Amir return to the party. Music. The fireworks continue, and the Ensemble enters, or unfreezes, now watching the impressive display overhead.

But Amir watches the following scene unfold: Hassan is standing down-

stage holding a silver platter of drinks. Assef approaches and takes one of
the drinks. He makes the gesture of a toast to Hassan, then smiles cruelly,
enjoying his position of power over him. He sips from the glass. Then
music as Assef and the Ensemble dance offstage. All exit except Amir.
Music fades out.

SCENE FOURTEEN

Baba's mansion and the bus station.

AMIR: If Hassan would leave, it would lessen his suffering. And mine, too. And I knew what I had to do.

Beat.

Baba bought me two birthday presents: a Schwinn Stingray—the king of all bicycles—and a gold wristwatch. Most of my relatives just sent cash. The night after my birthday, I told Baba I couldn't find my new watch anywhere. And the next morning, I grabbed my watch and a handful of cash, and I tiptoed across the garden to Hassan and Ali's shack. I lifted Hassan's mattress and planted the watch and cash under it. Then I told Baba what I hoped would be the last in a long line of shameful lies.

Baba, Ali, and Hassan enter.

BABA: That's it! I've had enough! We're going to get to the bottom of this and settle this thing once and for all. Now, Hassan, did you steal Amir's watch and that money? (*Pause.*) Well, did you?

HASSAN: (*pause*) Yes, I stole them.

Baba considers this for a moment.

BABA: That's okay, Hassan. I forgive you.

AMIR: (*to us*) Forgive? But if Baba could forgive that, why couldn't he forgive me for not being the son he always wanted?

BABA: Now, go play outside, boys.

ALI: We are leaving, Agha sahib.

BABA: What?

ALI: We are leaving. We cannot stay here anymore.

BABA: But I forgive him, Ali.

ALI: Life here is impossible for us now.

BABA: What do you mean, "life here is impossible"? (*Taking Ali aside, so the boys might not hear.*) Listen to me: I don't care about the watch or the cash.

ALI: I'm sorry, but our bags are packed. We've made our decision, Agha sahib.

BABA: You're serious.

ALI: Yes.

BABA: But haven't I provided well for you?

ALI: You have.

BABA: You're the brother I never had.

ALI: Please don't make this more difficult than it already is.

BABA: But I don't understand why you would leave.

ALI: Will you drive us to the bus station?

BABA: At least tell me why!

ALI: (*putting his arm around Hassan in a protective gesture*) We must leave here, Agha sahib.

BABA: No! I forbid it. Do you hear me, Ali? I forbid you to leave!

ALI: (*calmly*) Respectfully, you cannot forbid us anything, Agha sahib. We don't work for you anymore.

BABA: (*pause, as Baba realizes he has lost*) But where will you go?

ALI: To stay with my cousin in Hazarajat. Now, will you please take us to the bus station?

AMIR: (*to us*) Then I understood. This was Hassan's final sacrifice for me. If he'd said no, he didn't steal the watch or the cash, Baba would've believed him because Hassan never lied. Then *I'd* be revealed for what I really was and Baba would never forgive me. And that led to another understanding. Hassan *knew*. He knew I'd seen everything in that alley, and that I'd stood there and done nothing. He knew I had betrayed him, and yet, he was rescuing me once again.

BABA: If that's what you want. Get your things, and I'll get out the car.

AMIR: It rarely rained in the summer in Kabul. But it rained the afternoon Baba took Ali and Hassan to the bus station.

Over the following passage, the Ensemble enters upstage as passengers wait to board a bus. Ali and Hassan join the end of the line, with Ali holding a single suitcase and Hassan carrying a canvas bag slung over his shoulder and the cowboy hat Baba gave him for his birthday.

I watched them haul their bags to Baba's black Mustang. At the station, Baba did something I'd never seen him do before: he cried. I wondered how and when I'd become capable of causing this kind of pain. He stood by, hoping Ali would change his mind. Then, one by one, the passengers boarded the bus.

The passengers start to exit. Hassan takes a few steps and then stops and

*turns back toward Amir. They look at each other. Then Hassan turns
away and exits behind Ali.*

I caught one final glimpse of Hassan as the bus pulled away,
taking with it the boy whose first spoken word was my name.

*Baba exits in the other direction. Amir remains onstage alone as the lights
fade.*

End of Act One.

Act Two

SCENE ONE

Several refugees, as many of the Ensemble members as possible, including Baba, sit in the empty tank of a moving fuel truck. A Husband and Wife cradle a baby. Amir stands to the side.

AMIR: In 1978, communists in the Afghan army pulled off a military coup. President Daoud Khan was executed and Afghanistan was on the verge of civil war. Then in December 1979, the Soviet army invaded and all hell broke loose. With Russian soldiers patrolling the sidewalks and tanks rolling up and down the streets, Baba made the painful decision to leave.

Amir joins the others in the truck.

We hired a people smuggler to take us to Pakistan. A dangerous crossing in the tank of a fuel truck. (*Now as if reliving the events.*) It was pitch-black. It stank of shit, vomit, and gasoline. The air was thick, almost solid. You open your mouth and order your lungs to draw air. Now, you need air, need it NOW, but your lungs, they ignore you. They collapse, tighten, squeeze . . . panic sets in!

BABA: Think of something good, Amir. Think of something happy.

AMIR: Hassan . . . For you, a thousand times over.

First Russian Soldier enters. He carries an AK–47 slung over his shoulder.

FIRST RUSSIAN SOLDIER: Ei, stop the truck! A-stan-na-VEE ma-SHEEN-u! [*Stop the truck!*] Stop the truck!

He shines his flashlight in at the refugees.

Everybody out! Out of the truck! Vwee kha-DEE-tyeh! [*Get out!*]

Over the next line, the refugees get out of the truck.

Da-VAI-tyeh! Da-VAI-tyeh! [*Come on! Come on!*] Bis-STRAY-e! [*Faster!*] Vwee kha-DEE-tyeh! [*Get out!*] Ya ska-ZAL [*I said*], get out! Da-VAI-tyeh! [*Come on!*]

The refugees are out of the truck now.

Na ZEM-lyu! See-CHAS-jhe! [*On the ground! Now!*]

The refugees don't move; they don't understand him.

Sit down! On the ground! Sa-DEES! [*Sit!*]

Quickly, the refugees sit. The First Russian Soldier looks over the refugees. He gestures to the Woman with the baby.

I want thirty minutes, that woman. Now, get up. Come with me!

HUSBAND: Wait, no, what are you doing?

FIRST RUSSIAN SOLDIER: She price letting you pass. (*To the Woman.*) Ve-sta-VAI! [*Stand!*]

HUSBAND: No, don't do this.

FIRST RUSSIAN SOLDIER: Shut up!

HUSBAND: I'll pay you. How much do you want?

FIRST RUSSIAN SOLDIER: Don't want money. Want her.

HUSBAND: Please, show a little mercy—

FIRST RUSSIAN SOLDIER: (*ignoring the Husband*) Stand up, come with me!

HUSBAND: Maybe you have a wife or a mother—

FIRST RUSSIAN SOLDIER: (*to the Husband*) Zad-ke-NEES! [*Shut up!*] (*To the Woman as he grabs her arm.*) Now, stand up. See-CHAS-jhe! [*Now!*]

BABA: (*standing, to the Woman*) No. Don't move. (*To the First Russian Soldier.*) Where's your shame?

FIRST RUSSIAN SOLDIER: No shame in war.

BABA: You're wrong. War doesn't negate decency. It *demands* it, even more than in times of peace.

AMIR: Baba, sit down, you're going to get us all killed!

FIRST RUSSIAN SOLDIER: Better listen to boy.

BABA: No, you let us pass.

FIRST RUSSIAN SOLDIER: (*preparing his AK-47*) Will be good to put bullet in you.

BABA: I'll take a thousand bullets before I let this indecency take place.

AMIR: Baba, please!

The First Russian Soldier points his gun at Baba's chest.

BABA: You'd better kill me with that first shot.

The loud sound of a gunshot. But Baba remains standing. A Second Russian Soldier enters with his still-smoking gun held high.

SECOND RUSSIAN SOLDIER: Shto tee DEL-esh?! [*What are you doing?!*]

The First Russian Soldier lowers his gun.

FIRST RUSSIAN SOLDIER: Nee-chef-VOH. [*Nothing.*]

SECOND RUSSIAN SOLDIER: A-tai-ye-DEE aht syu-DAH. [*Get out of here.*] Bis-TRA! [*Now!*]

FIRST RUSSIAN SOLDIER: Da, Co-man-DEER. Ez-ven-EE-tyeh. [*Yes, Comrade. Excuse me.*]

First Russian Soldier exits.

SECOND RUSSIAN SOLDIER: (*to the refugees in the truck*) I apologize his behavior. Russia sends them here to fight, and when they come, they find pleasure of drug. I am sorry. Now, move along.

Second Russian Soldier exits.

AMIR: Baba scared me that night, but I had never been more proud.

The refugees exit.

By the time we arrived at the refugee camp in Pakistan, one of our group had suffocated and another committed suicide. But *we* made it.

Baba and Amir stand side by side, facing out, with two suitcases at Baba's feet.

After everything Baba built, fought for, and dreamed over, this was the summation of his life: two suitcases and one disappointing son. Six months later, our refugee applications were approved, and we were sent to America.

SCENE TWO

The San Francisco Bay Area, 1981. Amir takes a step downstage, as if stepping into the United States.

AMIR: San Francisco, California, 1981.

Music: Kool and the Gang's "Celebration." The Ensemble enters in eighties clothing and dances across the stage. Baba continues to stand center stage, looking out of place. As many members of the Ensemble as possible should be used for this scene with the lines divided accordingly.

AMIR: I marveled at the sheer size of America!

1980S AMERICAN #1: Beyond every city, another city!

1980S AMERICAN #2: Hills beyond mountains!

1980S AMERICAN #3: Mountains beyond hills!

1980S AMERICAN #4: Beyond those, more cities!

1980S AMERICAN #5: San Francisco!

1980S AMERICAN #6: Oakland!

1980S AMERICAN #7: San José!

1980S AMERICAN #1: Freeways beyond freeways!

1980S AMERICAN #2: BMWs!

1980S AMERICAN #3: Cadillacs!

1980S AMERICAN #4: Porsches!

AMIR: Cars I'd never seen in Afghanistan!

1980S AMERICAN #5: Baseball!

1980S AMERICAN #6: Football!

1980S AMERICAN #7: Basketball!

1980S AMERICAN #1: *Pac-Man!*

1980S AMERICAN #2: *Donkey Kong!*

1980S AMERICAN #3: *Dynasty!*

1980S AMERICAN #4: *Dallas!*

1980S AMERICAN #5: Darth Vader!

1980S AMERICAN #6: The Space Shuttle!

1980S AMERICAN #7: McDonald's!

1980S AMERICAN #1: Burger King!

1980S AMERICAN #2: Kool and the Gang!

1980S AMERICAN #3: Blondie!

1980S AMERICAN #4: Prince!

ENSEMBLE: I WANT MY MTV!!!

The Ensemble continues to dance as the music plays. Amir, though a little uncertain, allows the music to move his body. The music fades out as the Ensemble exits.

AMIR: America was a river, roaring along, unmindful of the past. I embraced America because I could wade into that river, let my sins drown to the bottom.

Beat.

Baba loved the *idea* of America. But it was living in America that gave him an ulcer.

Some Kid on Skateboard rides across the stage, almost collides with Baba.

BABA: The traffic gives me a headache. The smog stings my eyes. In this country, even the flies are pressed for time.

AMIR: And he hated Jimmy Carter.

BABA: (*to Amir*) Don't talk about Jimmy Carter! (*To us.*) Jimmy Carter's a big-toothed cretin! Done more for communism than Brezhnev. What America and the world need is a man to be reckoned with!

AMIR: That man came in the form of Ronald Reagan. And when Reagan called the Soviet Union "the Evil Empire," Baba went out and bought a Reagan/Bush bumper sticker.

Baba holds his suitcase high over his head and proudly reveals a Reagan/ Bush bumper sticker attached to the side.

BABA: (*to us*) Fuck the Russia! I love USA!

AMIR: Baba was the lone Republican in our building. And even though he was eligible to receive food stamps, he refused them.

BABA: (*to Amir*) I don't like it, charity money.

With the attitude of moving in, Baba strikes the suitcases offstage or somewhere on the set.

AMIR: So he got a job at a gas station working twelve-hour shifts six days a week.

SCENE THREE

Mrs. Nguyen's grocery store. Mrs. Nguyen enters and Baba approaches her.

AMIR: Across the street was a little grocery store run by a Vietnamese woman, Mrs. Nguyen. One day, Baba went in to buy some oranges.

BABA: (*as if in mid-argument*) What are you talking about?!

MRS. NGUYEN: But, sir, I need to see ID.

BABA: You don't trust me?!

MRS. NGUYEN: Sir, it policy!

BABA: I don't care about your damn policy!

AMIR: (*approaching Baba and Mrs. Nguyen*) What's going on?

BABA: (*to Amir*) I don't have any cash, so I wrote her a check!

MRS. NGUYEN: And I need to see ID!

BABA: Can you believe that?!

AMIR: Baba, it's not personal.

BABA: We buy her damn fruits, put money in her pocket, and now she wants to see my license!

AMIR: They're supposed to ask for ID.

MRS. NGUYEN: (*to Baba*) I don't want you here. (*To Amir.*) You, you nice man, but your father, he crazy. Not welcome anymore.

BABA: Does she think I'm a thief?

MRS. NGUYEN: I call police!

BABA: What kind of country is this? No one trusts anybody!

MRS. NGUYEN: You get out or I call police!

AMIR: Mrs. Nguyen, please. Please, don't call the police. I'll take him home, okay?

MRS. NGUYEN: Yes, you take him home. Good idea.

AMIR: Baba, promise me you won't go in there anymore.

BABA: Fine. I wouldn't want to go into that (*so Mrs. Nguyen can hear him*) donkey's store anyway! (*To Amir.*) See you at home.

Baba exits.

AMIR: (*to Mrs. Nguyen*) I'm sorry.

MRS. NGUYEN: ID for check is policy.

AMIR: I know. My father is still adjusting to America. In Afghanistan, we used a tree branch as a credit card. We'd take the stick down to the bread maker, and he'd carve a notch onto it for each loaf of naan. Then we'd pay him for the number of notches on the stick. No ID.

MRS. NGUYEN: Well . . . okay . . . You take care of him.

Mrs. Nguyen exits.

SCENE FOUR

AMIR: In 1983, I graduated from high school. I was by far the oldest senior tossing his mortarboard that day.

Baba enters carrying Amir's mortarboard.

BABA: Amir, ma iftikhar maykonom. I'm proud of you.

Baba shakes Amir's hand.

AMIR: (*to us*) Thanks, Baba.

BABA: Let's walk a little.

AMIR: Why?

BABA: Just come. There's something I want to show you.

They continue walking.

There. A Ford Gran Torino. Needs painting, and I'll have one of the guys at the station put in new shocks, but it runs.

Baba holds the keys out to Amir.

You'll need it to go to college in the fall.

AMIR: Thank you, Baba!

BABA: Want to try it out?

They get in the car.

AMIR: (*to us*) We drove the car around the block, testing the brakes, the radio, the turn signals. Then we just sat there. (*To Baba.*) It runs great, Baba.

BABA: I'm glad you like it.

Beat.

I wish Hassan had been with us today.

AMIR: Me too.

BABA: What's the name of that college again?

AMIR: San José State.

BABA: And what do you plan on majoring in?

AMIR: I think I'll major in creative writing.

BABA: Stories, you mean. They pay for that, making up stories?

AMIR: If you're good. And you get discovered.

BABA: How likely is that, getting discovered?

AMIR: It happens.

BABA: And what will you do while you wait to get good and get discovered?

AMIR: I'll find a job.

BABA: Oh, wa wa [*great*], so you'll study for years to earn a degree, then you'll get a chatti job like mine, one you could just as easily land today, on the small chance that your degree might someday

help you get *discovered*. You should do real work. Medical school.
Law school.

*Amir doesn't respond. Baba gets out of the car, tosses the mortarboard onto
the seat, and exits.*

AMIR: I felt guilty for indulging myself at the expense of his ulcer,
but I would stand my ground.

SCENE FIVE

The San José flea market. The Steve Miller Band's "Abracadabra" as the
flea market is established. Two flea market stands are needed here: one for
Amir and Baba, and the other for General Taheri and Soraya. The second
of these stands, the one belonging to General Taheri and Soraya, has
slightly higher-end items on it. On this stand, there should also be a cup of
tea. Soraya sits at her stand reading Jane Eyre. *The Ensemble enters.*
They mill about, looking at the things for sale on the stands: old records,
baseball gloves, wooden tennis rackets, stuffed animals, dolls, commemo-
rative glasses and plates, used books, a guitar . . . Over the following
passage, Baba and General Taheri enter and greet each other.

AMIR: In the summer of 1984, Baba and I would go to garage sales
and buy things people no longer wanted. Then we drove to the
San José flea market, rented a spot, and sold the junk for a small
profit. In those days, Afghan families worked an entire section
of the flea market.

BABA: Amir, I want you to meet somebody.

AMIR: Yes, Baba.

BABA: This is General Sahib, Mr. Iqbal Taheri. He worked for the
Ministry of Defense in Kabul.

AMIR: Salaam, General Sahib.

GENERAL TAHERI: Salaam, bachem [*my child*].

BABA: Amir is going to be a great writer. He just finished his first year of college and earned A's in all of his courses.

GENERAL TAHERI: Mashallah. [*Wonderful.*] Will you be writing about our country, history perhaps? Economics?

AMIR: I write fiction.

GENERAL TAHERI: (*with disdain*) Ah. A storyteller. Well, people need stories, too, to divert them at difficult times like this. Speaking of stories, your father and I hunted pheasant together one summer day in Jalalabad. If I recall correctly, your father's eye proved as keen in the hunt as it had in business.

BABA: I am not much of a businessman anymore—selling used tennis rackets and Barbie dolls.

GENERAL TAHERI: (*putting his hand on Baba's shoulder and speaking to Amir*) I have heard many men foolishly labeled great. Your father has the distinction of belonging to the minority who truly deserves the label.

BABA: You're flattering me.

GENERAL TAHERI: I am not. Boys and girls must know the legacies of their fathers. Do you appreciate your father, bachem?

AMIR: I do.

GENERAL TAHERI: Then congratulations. You are *halfway* to being a man.

Soraya notices that her father has left his tea on the stand. She picks up the cup and walks over to him.

SORAYA: Padar jan, your tea.

GENERAL TAHERI: (*as he takes the cup of tea from Soraya*) You are so kind, my dear. My daughter, Soraya jan.

Soraya and Amir hold eye contact. They don't see anyone except each other. Love at first sight.

SORAYA: Hello.

AMIR: (*taking a step toward her*) Hi.

GENERAL TAHERI: (*noticing the look between them*) Time to tend to our booth. Come on, Soraya.

Soraya and General Taheri return to their stand.

BABA: Be careful, Amir.

AMIR: Of what?

BABA: That man is Pashtun to the root. He has honor and pride, *nang* and *namoos,* the tenets of Pashtun men.

AMIR: Don't worry, Baba.

BABA: Especially when it comes to the chastity of his daughter.

AMIR: I said don't worry.

BABA: His wife died and his daughter is all he has left. Just don't embarrass me, Amir, that's all I ask.

AMIR: I won't. God, Baba.

Baba exits.

But after I met Soraya Taheri, I couldn't get her out of my mind.

The following sequence can be done with or without musical underscore. If music: consider Van Morrison's "Brown Eyed Girl." General Taheri exits and Soraya manages the flea market stand while Amir gazes at her, transfixed. Two members of the Ensemble come to purchase things from Amir's stand, but he is watching Soraya too intently to pay attention to them. One of them takes the opportunity to steal a few books. They run offstage. Soraya, meanwhile, goes from manning her stand to sitting on a bench, now reading Wuthering Heights. *She is beautiful and statuesque. If no music, cut the stealing of the books and the gazing, and just go to Amir's next line.*

For a month, I'd walk down the aisle of the flea market, repeatedly passing the Taheris' stand.

If music, continue. Amir walks casually past Soraya. She looks up and they make brief, furtive eye contact. Then Amir checks his watch. Soraya looks back down at her book. He walks past her again, going the other way, still trying to be casual, but hoping she will notice him. Music fades out, if used.

And that's all I did. But I promised myself I'd talk to her before the summer was over.

Amir nervously approaches Soraya.

Salaam.

SORAYA: (*looking up from her book*) Salaam.

AMIR: I'm sorry, I didn't mean to disturb you.

SORAYA: That's okay.

AMIR: Is General Sahib here today?

SORAYA: He went that way.

AMIR: Oh, okay. Will you tell him I stopped by to pay my respects?

SORAYA: I will.

AMIR: Thanks. Oh, and my name is Amir. In case you need to know.

SORAYA: Okay.

AMIR: So you can tell him, I mean. That I stopped by. To, uh, you know, pay my respects—

SORAYA: Got it: Amir.

AMIR: I guess I'll go now. Sorry to disturb you.

SORAYA: You didn't.

AMIR: Oh . . . good. (*Pause.*) Well, khoda hafez [*goodbye*].

SORAYA: Khoda hafez.

Amir starts to move away then . . .

AMIR: Can I ask what you're reading?

SORAYA: *Wuthering Heights.*

AMIR: It's a sad story.

SORAYA: Sad stories make good books.

AMIR: They do.

SORAYA: I heard *you* write.

AMIR: Would you like to read one of my—

SORAYA: Yes. I'd like that.

AMIR: Maybe I'll bring one someday.

SORAYA: Okay.

AMIR: Okay! Well, goodbye.

SORAYA: Bye.

AMIR: (*to us*) Every day, I'd wait until the general went for a stroll then I'd walk to the Taheris' stand. It went on like that for weeks.

Amir sits next to Soraya on the bench.

SORAYA: (*as if in mid-sentence*) . . . and so I'm taking classes at community college so I can be an English teacher. My father says anyone can teach. I know it doesn't pay much here, but it's what I want.

AMIR: Look, I brought you something.

He takes out several sheets of paper and gives them to Soraya.

As promised.

SORAYA: Oh, you remembered. Tashakor! [*Thank you!*]

AMIR: It's called *A Season for Ashes*. By me.

He waits a beat to see if she responds.

Here . . .

Amir moves closer and, looking over her shoulder, starts to read from the pages.

"Professor Morgan usually took the train to work, but on this particular morning, he decided to drive. As he stepped out into the warm California sunshine, he thought he saw—"

Without either noticing, General Taheri has come up behind them.

GENERAL TAHERI: Ah, Amir! Our aspiring storyteller.

Amir jumps up.

GENERAL TAHERI: What a pleasure.

AMIR: Salaam, General Sahib.

GENERAL TAHERI: It's a beautiful day. They say it will rain this week. Hard to believe, isn't it?

General Taheri holds out his hand. Soraya gives him the pages.

GENERAL TAHERI: You are a decent boy, but even decent boys need reminding sometimes. So it is my duty to remind you that you are among peers in this flea market. People talk. You see, everyone here is a storyteller.

General Taheri tears up the pages and gives them back to Amir.

Do pass my respects to your father, Amir jan.

AMIR: I will, General Sahib.

GENERAL TAHERI: Come on, Soraya.

Amir and Soraya share one more glance as she exits with her father.

SCENE SIX

AMIR: I didn't get to brood too much over what happened because Baba got sick. He collapsed at the flea market. His arms and legs were jerking. He was frothing at the mouth. I knelt beside him and felt a wetness on my knee. His bladder had let go. Later that day, the doctor showed me Baba's CAT scan. His brain was covered with little gray spots. Cancer. After weeks of paperwork and lost referrals, we finally got in to see the oncologist.

A medical clinic exam room. Baba enters, coughing. He sits on a patient's table.

BABA: I don't know what this doctor is going to tell me that I don't already know.

AMIR: He might be able to help you feel better, Baba.

BABA: I feel fine, Amir.

Dr. Schneider enters. A sunny attitude.

DR. SCHNEIDER: Hello, I'm Dr. Schneider.

AMIR: Hi.

DR. SCHNEIDER: (*to Baba*) Now, it doesn't look good, but we do have some options. We'll keep you on steroids to reduce the swelling in your brain, and we should start radiation. I'd also recommend—

Baba has a violent coughing fit.

DR. SCHNEIDER: Let's take a listen to that cough.

Dr. Schneider takes out his stethoscope and approaches Baba.

BABA: Wait, where are you from?

DR. SCHNEIDER: I'm sorry?

BABA: I said, where are you from?

DR. SCHNEIDER: Well, I grew up in Michigan, did med school in Ann Arbor, and then came out to San Francisco for my residency.

BABA: No, I don't mean that. I mean where's your family from?

DR. SCHNEIDER: Russia, originally.

BABA: Russia! No Russian is going to touch me!

Baba pushes Dr. Schneider away.

DR. SCHNEIDER: But, sir, I—

BABA: Get away from me!

AMIR: (*to Dr. Schneider*) I'm sorry. Can you give us a minute?

DR. SCHNEIDER: Of course. Take as much time as you need. I'll just be outside.

As Dr. Schneider exits, Amir takes Baba aside.

AMIR: Baba, I read his biography in the waiting room. He was born in *Detroit.*

BABA: I don't care.

AMIR: But he's more American than you and I will ever be.

BABA: No, he's *Roussi!* His parents were *Roussi,* his grandparents were *Roussi!* He's *Roussi!*

AMIR: His family *fled* from the Soviets. Like us!

BABA: I swear on your mother's face I'll break his arm if he tries to touch me.

AMIR: Baba, be reasonable, you can't—

BABA: Don't challenge me, Amir! Not on this. Now, get me another doctor.

Baba exits.

AMIR: The next oncologist, Dr. Amani, was Iranian, and Baba approved. But Baba's prognosis wasn't good. The cancer had started in his lungs and spread to his brain. Nothing could be done. Baba refused radiation. Over the next few days, our apartment was jammed with Afghans wishing Baba a speedy recovery. And that included, of course, General Taheri and Soraya. Later that week, I asked Baba to call on the general to ask for his daughter's hand. The general accepted my proposal, but Soraya insisted on meeting with me first.

SCENE SEVEN

SORAYA: (*entering*) Amir?

AMIR: Salaam.

SORAYA: Salaam. Listen . . . I need to tell you something. I don't want us to start with any secrets, and I'd rather you hear it from me.

AMIR: Okay.

SORAYA: (*pause*) When we were living in Virginia, before my mother died . . . I ran away with an Afghan man. He was into drugs, and I was young and rebellious . . . and stupid. We lived together for a month. All the Afghans were talking about it. Then my father found us. He showed up one night with a gun. Said he had two bullets in the chamber—one for the man and one for himself if I didn't come home. I kept saying he couldn't keep me locked up forever, saying I hated him, I wished he was dead. He brought me home yelling and screaming, calling him all kinds of names. He took me up to my bedroom, handed me a pair of scissors, and told me to cut off all my hair.

Beat.

When my mother saw me, she was sitting on the sofa, crying so hard she couldn't get up. She just sat there, tears running down her face, slurring her words. We didn't know it then, but she'd had a stroke. Six months later, she passed away.

Beat.

Then my father and I moved to California.

AMIR: I'm sorry.

SORAYA: It's okay.

AMIR: How are you and your father now?

SORAYA: We've always had our differences. But, you know, I'm grateful he came for me that night. He saved me.

Beat.

So does that bother you?

AMIR: A little.

SORAYA: Enough to change your mind?

AMIR: No, Soraya. Not even close. Nothing you said changes how I feel about you.

SORAYA: That was years ago and thousands of miles away, and I still hear people talking about it.

AMIR: Fuck 'em.

SORAYA: I was sure you'd change your mind.

AMIR: No chance of that, Soraya. I want us to marry.

They share a smile.

But you'd better go, or your father will be coming after *me*.

SORAYA: Yeah, I should.

Soraya starts to exit.

AMIR: Soraya?

SORAYA: Yes?

AMIR: I have, uh . . . never mind. Thanks for coming.

After one last shared look, Soraya exits.

I almost told her about Hassan. . . . There are many reasons Soraya Taheri is a better person than me. Courage is just one of them.

SCENE EIGHT

A banquet hall. Afghan wedding music: ahesta boro.

AMIR: Baba spent the remainder of his life savings on our wedding.
He rented the banquet hall, bought my tuxedo, her gown, and
the diamond ring. Paid for my traditional green suit, the color of
Islam, for the swearing ceremony.

*The music continues to play. Soraya enters, followed by General Taheri,
Baba, who now walks with the aid of a cane, and the Ensemble. She and
Amir re-create the movements of a bride and groom in an Afghan wed-
ding ceremony. They link arms and slowly walk downstage. General
Taheri walks next to Soraya and Baba walks next to Amir, while the rest
of the Ensemble follows behind. Someone holds a Koran over Amir and
Soraya.*

*A small sofa is brought out and placed behind them, and they sit side by
side, like royalty, facing the audience. A table is placed in front of them.
On the table is a combination of food, flowers, gifts, and materials for
painting henna. General Taheri stands to one side, Baba to the other. The
rest of the Ensemble gathers around.*

*The member of the Ensemble who holds the Koran kisses it lightly and
taps it to his forehead. He then gives it to Soraya, who does the same. She
hands it to Amir, who repeats the gesture.*

Two members of the Ensemble then pull a large green veil up and over

Amir and Soraya. The veil should create the sense of intimacy, a space concealed from the view of the Ensemble, though not from the audience.

AMIR: (*to us*) Then we were served sharbat and malida, and henna was put on our hands.

Another member of the Ensemble brings Amir and Soraya a mirror. They hold the mirror in front of them and gaze into it as if seeing each other anew. Somewhat self-consciously and a little shyly, they smile.

AMIR: (*to us*) As I gazed into Soraya's eyes, I wondered if Hassan too had married. And if so, whose eyes he gazed into, whose hands he held?

Amir allows his gaze to return to the mirror.

The music shifts to Afghan dance music. The ensemble cheers and yells, "YAY!" The sofa, table, sheet, mirror, and any other remnants from the wedding are removed and everyone dances to the music, with the exception of General Taheri and Baba. There is laughter, clapping, gaiety, and some showing off. During this, Baba exits, unnoticed.

Around two a.m., the party moved to Baba's apartment! Tea flowed and music played until the neighbors called the cops!

The music stops. All exit in a run, except Amir.

SCENE NINE

Baba's apartment.

AMIR: Soraya moved in with Baba and me. She said getting our own place was out of the question, what with Baba as sick as he was.

Baba, who now sits in a wheelchair, is brought on by Soraya.

She helped Baba in and out of bed, and cooked his favorite dish, potato shorwa. She gave him his medication, washed his clothes, and every night, she read to him.

Soraya reads from a leather-bound book, the same one Rahim Khan gave Amir on his birthday in Kabul.

SORAYA: "But he was a happy man and rarely shed a tear. So he found ways to make himself sad so his tears could make him rich. One day—"

AMIR: (*as if walking in, putting keys back in his pocket*) Hey, what are you reading him that for?

SORAYA: I'm sorry, Amir, I—

AMIR: Where did you find it?

SORAYA: I didn't think it'd be—

BABA: I put her up to it.

AMIR: What?

BABA: I asked her to read it.

AMIR: You did?

BABA: I hope you don't mind.

AMIR: No, of course, I don't mind.

SORAYA: (*to Baba*) I'll get your pills and a glass of water.

BABA: No. Not tonight. There is no pain tonight. I'd just like to go
     to bed.

SORAYA: Okay. Bia [*Come*], Baba jan.

She starts to wheel him away.

BABA: Wait.

*Weakly, Baba stands. He faces Amir. Then Baba embraces Amir in a hug.
This should be only the second time we see them hug each other (the first
being after the kite tournament). Then Baba pulls back, so they can look at
each other.*

     Good night, Amir.

AMIR: Good night, Baba.

*Amir and Soraya help Baba back into the wheelchair. Baba and Soraya
exit.*

     Baba went to sleep that night and never woke up. We buried him
     in the Afghan section of a local cemetery. He had wrestled bears
     his whole life. Losing his wife. Raising a son by himself. Leaving
     his homeland. Poverty. Indignity. In the end, a bear had come he
     couldn't beat. But even then, he lost on his own terms.

SCENE TEN

Five years later. Amir and Soraya's house in San Francisco.

AMIR: In the summer of 1989, five years after Baba's death, I published my first novel. Soraya and I bought a house in San Francisco and we settled into the routine of married life. She found a job teaching elementary school. I wrote books. We couldn't have children because Soraya had something called "Unexplained Infertility." I remember breaking the news to her father.

Soraya enters with General Taheri in mid-conversation.

SORAYA: . . . and so the doctor said we could adopt.

GENERAL TAHERI: Oh, he did, did he?

SORAYA: He said it was an option.

GENERAL TAHERI: (*to Amir, accusingly*) And you're going to do that? Adopt a child?

AMIR: (*to General Taheri*) No. (*To Soraya.*) I don't know, maybe. (*Back to General Taheri.*) Probably not.

GENERAL TAHERI: Just as well. This adoption thing, I'm not so sure it's for us Afghans anyway. For one thing, children want to know who their natural parents are. Blood is a powerful thing, never forget that.

SORAYA: I don't want to talk about this anymore—

GENERAL TAHERI: Take Amir, here. We all knew his father. I know
who his grandfather was in Kabul and his great-grandfather before him. That's why when his father came, I didn't hesitate.

SORAYA: But, Baba—

GENERAL TAHERI: And believe me, his father wouldn't have agreed
to ask for you if he didn't know whose descendant *you* were.

SORAYA: Baba, please—

GENERAL TAHERI: (*rising to a conclusion*) When you adopt, you do
not know whose blood you're bringing into your house! What
do *you* think, Amir?

Pause. Soraya folds her arms.

SORAYA: Yes, what *do* you think, Amir?

*Soraya and General Taheri look intently at Amir. He is caught in the
middle of their argument and has to choose a side. After a moment:*

AMIR: I think you're right, General.

SORAYA: (*angry that Amir has not taken her side*) I'm going to check
on dinner.

Soraya exits.

GENERAL TAHERI: (*to Amir*) Now, if you were American, it wouldn't
matter. People here marry for love. But we are Afghans. (*Notices
that Soraya has left the room.*) Soraya, come back here, I am talking
to you.

General Taheri exits after her.

AMIR: So we got a cocker spaniel instead. But sometimes, at night,
after we would roll to our separate sides of the bed, I could feel

her emptiness, as if a living, breathing thing had crept into our marriage.

Rahim Khan enters.

RAHIM KHAN: Come see me. There is a way to be good again.

AMIR: Then in June 2001, I got that phone call from Rahim Khan.

RAHIM KHAN: Please. Come see me.

AMIR: "A way to be good again." That told me he knew everything. I don't know how, but he *knew*. He knew about Assef, Hassan, the kite, the watch. I went for a walk in Golden Gate Park, saw that pair of kites, and when I got home, I told Soraya I was going to Pakistan.

SCENE ELEVEN

Peshawar, Pakistan. Summer 2001. The sound of a commercial jet flying overhead and then the sounds of a crowded city street.

AMIR: The last time I'd seen Rahim Khan was the night Baba and I fled Kabul.

Rahim Khan enters. He and Amir take a moment to see each other. Then they embrace in a hug.

It's good to see you.

RAHIM KHAN: Thank you for coming, Amir.

Rahim Khan looks much older now and has a full, scraggly beard.

AMIR: How did you find me?

RAHIM KHAN: It's not difficult to find people in America. I bought a map of the United States and called up information for cities in Northern California.

AMIR: You did?

RAHIM KHAN: It didn't take as long as you might think.

Rahim Khan coughs and holds a handkerchief to his mouth. He gestures for Amir to sit.

AMIR: (*to us, as they sit*) We talked for hours and I told him about Baba, the flea market, my books, and of course . . .

RAHIM KHAN: Soraya Taheri . . . that's a familiar name.

AMIR: She's General Taheri's daughter.

RAHIM KHAN: Ah, yes. And General Taheri has a brother, what's his name?

AMIR: Sharif jan.

RAHIM KHAN: Balay! [*Yes!*] I knew Sharif jan in Kabul.

AMIR: Right, he lives in America now. He's been working for the immigration service for years.

RAHIM KHAN: Do you and Soraya have children?

AMIR: No.

RAHIM KHAN: That's a shame.

AMIR: How are you? I mean really?

RAHIM KHAN: Truth is, not so good. I'm dying, Amir. I came to Pakistan to see a doctor. But there's no hope.

AMIR: How long?

RAHIM KHAN: A month. Maybe two.

AMIR: Let me take you back to America, I can find you a good doctor there and—

RAHIM KHAN: I have seen enough doctors. It's God's will. But that's not the reason I asked you to come. I want you to do something for me.

AMIR: Anything.

RAHIM KHAN: You know all those years I lived in your father's house after you left?

AMIR: Yeah . . .

RAHIM KHAN: Hassan lived there with me.

AMIR: Hassan?

RAHIM KHAN: I lived alone for the first five years. But by 1986, most of my friends and relatives had either been killed or had escaped. I barely knew anyone in Kabul, and God help me, I was lonely. So I went to Hazarajat to find Hassan. He was married and had befriended a Farsi teacher, who taught him to read and write.

AMIR: Was Ali with him?

RAHIM KHAN: No. Ali was killed in a land mine blast. You know, I don't think there's a more Afghan way to die than stepping on a mine.

Beat.

I asked Hassan and his wife to move to Kabul with me. The two of them did all the cooking and cleaning. Hassan tended the flowers, painted the walls. Then in 1990, Hassan's wife had a baby boy. They named him Sohrab, after Hassan's favorite hero from the *Shahnamah*. Here.

He takes out a picture and gives it to Amir.

The sweetest boy. Outside the walls of that house, there was a war raging. It was hell on earth. But the four of us made our own little haven from it. Hassan taught Sohrab how to read and write, and how to shoot the slingshot. By the time he was eight, he was deadly with that thing.

Amir starts to hand the picture back.

No, you keep that.

AMIR: Where's Hassan now?

RAHIM KHAN: Hassan would even take his son kite running. He would prop Sohrab on his shoulders and they would run through the streets. But when the Taliban took over, they banned kite flying.

AMIR: Rahim Khan, where's Hassan?

RAHIM KHAN: Soon after I came here to Pakistan, a rumor spread that a Hazara family was living alone in a big house in the Wazir Akbar Khan. A pair of Taliban officials came to investigate. They accused Hassan of lying when he told them he was living with me. The Talibs said he was a thief like all Hazaras and ordered him and his family to get out.

Talib Official #1, Talib Official #2, and Hassan enter. Hassan has a sack over his head.

When Hassan protested, they took him to the street.

Hassan drops to his knees.

And shot him in the back of the head.

Talib Official #1 shoots Hassan and Hassan falls forward.

AMIR: Oh, God. No.

RAHIM KHAN: When his wife came screaming, they shot her, too.

Talib Official #1 fires into the wings.

Self-defense, they claimed. Evicting a trespasser. And the Taliban moved into the house.

Hassan's body is removed. Alternatively, the shooting of Hassan could be played behind a screen in shadow.

AMIR: Hassan, I'm sorry. I'm so sorry.

RAHIM KHAN: Now, Amir, listen to me. This is what I want you to do. Sohrab is in an orphanage in Kabul. You must go to Kabul and bring him here.

AMIR: But I can't go to Kabul.

RAHIM KHAN: I know an American couple here in Pakistan. They run a charity home for Afghan children.

AMIR: You can't be serious.

RAHIM KHAN: Kabul is full of broken children. I don't want Sohrab to become another.

AMIR: But I don't want to go to Kabul, I can't!

RAHIM KHAN: We can give Sohrab a new life.

AMIR: Why me? Why can't you pay someone to go? If it's a matter of money, *I'll* pay for it.

RAHIM KHAN: It's not about money, Amir! And why you? I think we both know why it has to be you. If it wasn't for what you did, Hassan might be living in America now.

AMIR: But I have a wife, a home, a career. You'd have me risk all that for a kid I've never met and who might not even be—

RAHIM KHAN: Your father once told me, "A boy who won't stand up for himself becomes a man who can't stand up to anything." I wonder if that's what you've become.

AMIR: So maybe Baba was right.

RAHIM KHAN: I'm sorry you think that.

Beat.

But there's something else. Something you don't know.

AMIR: What?

RAHIM KHAN: Ali was sterile. He couldn't have children.

AMIR: Yes, he did. His wife had Hassan before she ran off.

RAHIM KHAN: But Ali wasn't Hassan's father.

AMIR: Then who was?

RAHIM KHAN: I think you know who.

AMIR: (*pause*) Baba?

Rahim Khan is silent.

You bastards. You goddamn bastards! All of you, you bunch of lying goddamn bastards!

RAHIM KHAN: Please, Amir.

AMIR: Did Hassan know?

RAHIM KHAN: Nobody knew.

AMIR: How could you hide this from me? From *him?*

RAHIM KHAN: It was a shameful situation. Your father, he loved you both, but he was torn between two halves. He could not love Hassan openly. People would talk.

AMIR: I don't need this shit.

RAHIM KHAN: So he took it out on you instead. He—

AMIR: My whole life has been one big fucking lie! What can you say? Nothing. Not a goddamn thing!

Amir starts to leave.

RAHIM KHAN: Please, Amir. Don't go.

Amir leaves the apartment.

AMIR: How could I have been so blind? The signs came flying back at me now: Baba never missing Hassan's birthday, Baba getting so upset when I asked if he'd consider getting new servants, the way he wept when Hassan and Ali left. And how had Ali lived in that house, knowing his master had betrayed him and fathered a child with his wife? Turned out Baba and I were more alike than I had known. We had both betrayed the people who would have given their lives for us.

Beat.

So Rahim Khan had summoned me here to atone not just for my sins but for Baba's, too. "A way to be good again." I went back and told Rahim Khan I was going to Kabul.

Rahim Khan nods and exits.

SCENE TWELVE

Farid enters. On the road from Peshawar to Kabul.

FARID: You Amir?

AMIR: (*checking the name on a piece of paper in his hand*) Yeah, you must be. . . .

FARID: Farid. My name's Farid.

AMIR: (*extending his hand*) Nice to meet you.

Farid does not take Amir's hand. Instead, he grunts an unfriendly hello.

FARID: Get in the car.

Farid goes to sit in the car.

AMIR: (*to us*) We drove west. And as we crossed into Afghanistan, reminders of the wars littered the road: burned-out carcasses of Soviet tanks, overturned trucks. (*To Farid.*) Are the Taliban as bad as I hear?

FARID: No, they're worse. They don't let you be human. They banned kite flying, music, alcohol. Women have to wear the burqa. I once saw a Talib beat a woman so hard, her mother's milk leaked out of her bones. They even execute people in the soccer stadium now.

Beat.

Hard to believe when the Taliban first rolled in, many of us danced in the street. They put an end to all the fighting. Peace at last. But at what price?

AMIR: Strange. I feel like a tourist in my own country.

FARID: You think of this as your country?

AMIR: I grew up in Afghanistan.

FARID: Let me guess. You lived in a big house with a garden. Your father drove an American car. You had servants, probably Hazaras. Am I close?

AMIR: Yes.

FARID: You've always been a tourist here.

Beat.

AMIR: (*to us*) When we entered Kabul, the poverty only got worse. Rubble and beggars everywhere. Collapsed buildings. Entire city blocks had been destroyed. (*To Farid.*) My father built an orphanage a little south of here.

FARID: Yeah, I remember that orphanage. The Taliban tore it down.

AMIR: (*looking around*) Where are all the trees?

FARID: Used for firewood. Besides, snipers used to hide in them. There's the new orphanage.

AMIR: (*to us, as they exit the car*) Didn't look so new. It was in a ruined barracks along the now dried-up Kabul River.

SCENE THIRTEEN

A rundown orphanage in Kabul. Zaman enters.

ZAMAN: Salaam alaykum.

AMIR: Walaykum salaam. We're searching for this boy.

Amir shows Zaman the picture of Sohrab.

His name is Sohrab.

ZAMAN: I am sorry. I have never seen that boy.

AMIR: But you barely looked at the picture—look again.

ZAMAN: I know every child in this institution and that one does not look familiar. Now, I have work to do.

AMIR: We don't mean any harm.

ZAMAN: I told you, he's not here. Go away.

AMIR: (*increasingly desperate*) I just want to take the boy to a safe place. I knew his father. Sohrab can read and write. And he's good with the slingshot. There's hope for this boy, Agha, a way out. Please.

ZAMAN: How do you know the boy's father?

AMIR: I'm his half brother.

ZAMAN: (*softening*) Well, you were wrong about one thing. That boy's *great* with the slingshot. Takes it everywhere he goes. Come in. We can talk in my office.

As they walk to Zaman's office . . .

FARID: How many orphans live here?

ZAMAN: More than we have room for. Many of them lost their fathers in the war, and their mothers can't feed them because the Taliban don't allow them to work, so they bring their children here. This place is better than the street, but not much.

Beat.

You say there is hope for your nephew? You may be too late.

AMIR: Just tell me where he is.

ZAMAN: There's a Talib official, visits once a month. He brings cash, not a lot, better than nothing. Then he takes a child.

AMIR: And you allow this?

ZAMAN: What choice do I have?

AMIR: But your job is to protect these children.

ZAMAN: And I do the best I can.

FARID: Cooney [*faggot*], you're selling *children!*

ZAMAN: There's nothing I can—

Farid lunges at Zaman.

FARID: You bastard! I'll kill you!

Amir steps in to stop the fight.

AMIR: Farid, let it go!

FARID: I'm going to kill him, the bastard!

AMIR: Come on, let it go!

Farid continues to pummel Zaman and shout insults, like mordagow [pimp], *cooney* [faggot], *padar lawnat* [bastard]. *Ad lib.*

Enough, Farid! *That's enough!*

Amir tries to separate Farid from Zaman.

Come on! Get off him!

Finally, Farid backs off.

ZAMAN: (*regaining his composure*) The Talib took Sohrab a month ago.

FARID: Mordagow, you're nothing but a fucking pimp!

ZAMAN: (*finally breaking*) I'm broke because I spent all I had on this godforsaken orphanage! I could have run like everyone else, to Pakistan or Iran, or maybe even America! But I *stayed!* I stayed because of the children! Yes, my job is to protect them, and that's exactly what I do. If I deny the Talib one, he takes ten. So I give him one and leave the judging to Allah. Then I take his goddamn filthy money and I buy food for the children!

AMIR: What happens to the ones he takes?

ZAMAN: Sometimes they come back. Sometimes they don't.

AMIR: And how do we find this man?

ZAMAN: (*he pulls out a paper from a pocket inside his coat*) I'll set up an appointment. Here's the address. (*He hands the paper to Amir.*) Now go.

Amir starts to speak.

Just go!

Zaman exits.

FARID: Why didn't you tell me the reason for your coming here?

AMIR: You didn't ask.

FARID: I used to have children myself. Two daughters. They were lost in the war. I will help you find this boy.

AMIR: Thank you, Farid. (*To us.*) Several hours later, we were standing in the driveway of a big house.

Amir and Farid stand side by side, facing the audience, as if looking at the house.

FARID: So I guess I'll wait for you in the car. See you in a few minutes, no?

AMIR: I hope so.

Farid exits.

SCENE FOURTEEN

A large home in Kabul. Two armed Guards enter. They guide Amir to sit in a chair.

Assef enters. He wears dark, John Lennon–style sunglasses, a long beard, and a white robe with drops of blood splattered on the sleeve and front. He tosses a brass ball in his hand. Amir does not recognize him.

ASSEF: Salaam.

AMIR: Salaam.

ASSEF: So you come from America?

AMIR: Yes.

ASSEF: You like it there?

AMIR: I'm looking for a boy.

ASSEF: A lot of people are looking for things they never find.

AMIR: I understand he's here. His name is Sohrab.

ASSEF: What I want to know is: What are you doing in America? Why aren't you here, with your Muslim brothers, serving your country?

AMIR: I've been away a long time.

ASSEF: There are those who believe abandoning your country when it needs you most is the same as treason. I could have you arrested and shot. Does that frighten you?

AMIR: I'm only here for the boy.

ASSEF: Answer me! Does that frighten you?

AMIR: Yes.

ASSEF: It should.

Sees that Amir notices the blood on his robe.

Excuse my appearance. I haven't had a chance to clean up since the show at the soccer stadium this afternoon. Bringing justice to another adulterer.

Beat.

Would you like to see the boy?

AMIR: What?

ASSEF: The boy. Would you like to see him?

AMIR: Yes.

ASSEF: *(to the Guards)* Go get him.

They exit.

Ah, but if you wanted to see a show, you should have been in Mazar-i-Sharif when we massacred the Hazaras. Door to door we went, calling for the men and boys. We'd shoot them right there in front of their families. Let them remember who they were, where they belonged. Sometimes, we went inside their homes. I'd sweep the barrel of my machine gun around the room and fire and fire until the smoke blinded me! You don't know the meaning of the word "liberating" until you've done that, stood in a roomful of targets, let the bullets fly! It's breathtaking! We left their bodies rotting in the streets like dogs. Dog meat for dogs. Now, that was a show.

AMIR: Some show. Massacring Hazaras in the name of Islam.

Pause, as Assef turns to face Amir.

ASSEF: You know, *Faggot*, I've often wondered whatever happened to old Flat-Nose.

Beat.

What did you think, you could waltz back here with your American ways, and I wouldn't recognize you?

Assef takes off his sunglasses.

AMIR: Assef?

ASSEF: Amir. It's been a long time.

AMIR: What are you doing here?

ASSEF: No, the question is what are *you* doing here?

AMIR: I told you.

ASSEF: The boy.

AMIR: Yes.

ASSEF: Why?

AMIR: I'll pay you for him. I can have money wired, how much—

ASSEF: Money?

He laughs.

I didn't fight the Soviets for money, and I didn't join the Taliban for money either. There are things traitors like you don't understand.

AMIR: Like what?

ASSEF: Like pride in your people, your customs, your language! Afghanistan is like a beautiful mansion littered with garbage, and someone has to take the garbage out!

AMIR: All I want is the boy.

ASSEF: "All I want is the boy." But why?

AMIR: I want to take him to a better place.

ASSEF: See, there's one thing I don't understand: Why would you come all the way from America for a Hazara? What makes *him* so special? Huh?

The Guards enter with Sohrab.

Why, look who it is. Stand up, Amir, I want you to meet somebody. My Hazara boy! (*Walking over to Sohrab.*) Now I have my own Hazara boy, just like your Hassan. Only mine is talented. (*To Sohrab.*) Show our guest what you can do.

One of the Guards pushes Play on a boom box. Pashtu music. Sohrab dances to it without interest, having done this before. Assef puts the brass ball down on a table. He and the Guards laugh and clap. When the music stops, Sohrab stops dancing.

How talented he is, my Hazara boy! (*To Amir.*) So you want him?

AMIR: Yes.

ASSEF: Very well, then. You can have him.

Pause.

Go on.

Amir takes a step toward Sohrab.

But I didn't say you could have him for free.

AMIR: What do you want?

ASSEF: You have to earn him. We have some unfinished business, you and I. (*To the Guards.*) Wait outside. No matter what you hear, don't come in. Only one of us will walk out of this room alive. If it's him, he's earned his freedom and you let him pass. Understand?

GUARD #1: But, Agha sahib—

ASSEF: Let him pass! And let the boy stay. Let him watch.

The Guards exit as Assef takes out a pair of brass knuckles.

I'm going to enjoy this.

Assef presses Play on the boom box. Loud Pashtu music. A violent fight between Assef and Amir with Assef getting in the majority of the blows. He is just about to finish the job when Sohrab pulls out his slingshot. He puts Assef's brass ball in the cup, pulls the cup back, and points it in the direction of Assef's face.

SOHRAB: Stop! No more!

Assef stops beating Amir. Turns toward Sohrab.

ASSEF: Put it down, Hazara—

SOHRAB: Please, stop hurting him!

ASSEF: —or what I'm doing to him will be nothing compared to what I'll do to you!

SOHRAB: Stop!

ASSEF: I said, PUT IT DOWN!

Assef lunges at Sohrab, who releases the slingshot. The brass ball hits Assef in the eye. He howls in pain.

Ahhhhhh!

SOHRAB: (*to Amir*) Let's go!

ASSEF: My eye! Get it out! *My eye!*

Assef continues to shout and howl in pain.

SOHRAB: Come on!

The Guards enter and rush Assef offstage. Music fades out.

SCENE FIFTEEN

AMIR: We stumbled to the car where, thank God, Farid was still waiting. Then I passed out. When I woke up, we were in Pakistan. My plan was to drop Sohrab off with Rahim Khan, then fly home. But when I went to find him, Rahim Khan was gone. And it turned out there was no American couple running a charity home for Afghan children. I didn't know what to do. So I called Soraya. I told her everything, about Hassan, the kite, the watch, Assef, Baba, Sohrab. By the time I was done, we were both crying.

SORAYA: You have to bring him home. He's family. You can't leave him on the streets.

AMIR: I know. . . .

SORAYA: I'll talk to some of my uncle's friends at the immigration service.

AMIR: And I'll see what the U.S. embassy can do.

SORAYA: Okay, ma dost et darom. [*I love you.*]

Amir and Sohrab play panjpar in a hotel room in Islamabad.

AMIR: Do you know who I am?

Sohrab nods.

Did your father ever tell you about me?

Sohrab nods.

What did he say?

SOHRAB: He said you were the best friend he ever had.

AMIR: I wasn't such a good friend, I'm afraid. But I'd like to be your friend. Would you like that?

SOHRAB: Yes.

AMIR: When we were growing up together, I'd read to him. His favorite story was of "Rostam and Sohrab." That's how you got your name.

SOHRAB: I know.

AMIR: Your father and I were brothers. Half brothers, really.

SOHRAB: He never said he had a brother.

AMIR: That's because he didn't know.

SOHRAB: Why didn't he know?

AMIR: No one told him. No one told me either. I just found out.

SOHRAB: Why didn't anyone tell you?

AMIR: Let's just say your father and I weren't supposed to be brothers.

Beat.

Listen, I live in San Francisco with my wife. Would you like to come live with us there?

SOHRAB: I saw a picture of San Francisco once. There was a red bridge and tall buildings.

AMIR: You should see the streets. They're so steep, when you drive up all you see is the hood of the car and the sky.

SOHRAB: That sounds scary.

AMIR: It is the first few times, but you get used to it.

SOHRAB: Does it snow there?

AMIR: No. But we get a lot of fog. You know that red bridge?

SOHRAB: Yes.

AMIR: Sometimes the fog is so thick, all you see is the top of the two towers poking through.

SOHRAB: Do many people speak Farsi?

AMIR: No, but my wife speaks Farsi. And you'll learn English fast.

SOHRAB: What if you get tired of me?

AMIR: I won't get tired of you, Sohrab.

SOHRAB: What if your wife doesn't like me?

AMIR: Trust me, Soraya is going to love you.

SOHRAB: I don't want to go to another orphanage.

AMIR: I won't ever let that happen.

SOHRAB: Please, promise you won't. Promise me.

AMIR: I promise, Sohrab. No orphanage. I promise.

SCENE SIXTEEN

A meeting room in the U.S. embassy. Omar Faisal enters in a rush carrying an overstuffed briefcase, a worn legal pad, and a handkerchief to mop the sweat from his forehead. His clothes are rumpled and loose-fitting. He is always running late.

OMAR FAISAL: Amir? Welcome to the U.S. embassy. Omar Faisal.

They shake hands.

AMIR: Nice to meet you.

Omar Faisal sets his briefcase down and begins riffling through the legal pad.

OMAR FAISAL: You too. I'm an immigration attorney and the embassy brings me in to consult on cases like yours. I know both sides of the equation pretty well. Born in Karachi, lived in Kabul, but actually, I grew up in Berkeley, California.

AMIR: Berkeley?

OMAR FAISAL: Yeah, my dad had a music store there in the sixties. I was even at Woodstock.

AMIR: Right.

OMAR FAISAL: You know what I'm talking about!

Omar Faisal high-fives Amir.

   Now, where did I put that pen . . . ?

Starts looking for the pen.

Raymond Andrews enters. He is carrying a file folder.

RAYMOND ANDREWS: Good afternoon.

OMAR FAISAL: *(to Amir)* Raymond Andrews. He handles visa re-
   quests.

AMIR: Hello.

RAYMOND ANDREWS: Hi. Look, I'll get right to the point. We've
   been reviewing your case, and my advice is to give it up.

AMIR: I'm sorry?

RAYMOND ANDREWS: Your petition to adopt this young fellow.
   Give it up.

AMIR: *(to Omar Faisal)* Really?

OMAR FAISAL: Well, not necessarily. If living in America has taught
   me anything, it's that giving up is right up there with pissing in
   the Girl Scouts' lemonade jar.

He laughs. The others don't and he cuts himself short.

   But it's our job to give you the facts. And truth is, you've got a
   tough battle ahead of you.

AMIR: Why?

RAYMOND ANDREWS: Your petition faces significant obstacles, not
   the least of which is that this child is not a legal orphan.

AMIR: Of course he is.

RAYMOND ANDREWS: No, legally, he's not.

AMIR: But his parents were executed in the street.

RAYMOND ANDREWS: You have death certificates?

AMIR: *Death certificates?* This is Afghanistan we're talking about. Most people there don't have *birth* certificates.

RAYMOND ANDREWS: I don't make the laws. You need to prove the parents are deceased, and the boy has to be declared a legal orphan.

AMIR: But how can I—

RAYMOND ANDREWS: Your next problem is you need the cooperation of the child's country of origin. That's difficult under the best of circumstances, and, to quote you, this is *Afghanistan* we're talking about.

AMIR: So I should throw him out, leave him for dead?

OMAR FAISAL: No one said that. We're just telling you how it works.

AMIR: But I'm his uncle, doesn't that count for anything?

RAYMOND ANDREWS: Does if you can prove it.

OMAR FAISAL: You got any papers or anyone who can attest to that?

AMIR: No, no papers. No one knew about it. And the one person who can support me is gone, maybe dead, I don't know.

OMAR FAISAL: Are you Muslim?

AMIR: Yes.

RAYMOND ANDREWS: Practicing?

AMIR: No.

RAYMOND ANDREWS: Doesn't help your case.

AMIR: So what are my options?

RAYMOND ANDREWS: You don't have any.

Raymond Andrews starts to leave.

OMAR FAISAL: Wait, wait, wait, wait, wait. There is one thing you can try, Amir. You could relinquish him to an orphanage here, return home, then file an orphan petition from the U.S.

AMIR: I can't do that.

OMAR FAISAL: Why not?

AMIR: I promised him I wouldn't send him back to an orphanage.

OMAR FAISAL: I'm sorry, but the orphanage is your best shot.

RAYMOND ANDREWS: Hell, I'd say it's your only shot.

Raymond Andrews exits.

OMAR FAISAL: Good luck, Amir.

Beat.

And about what you're trying to do, I think it's pretty great.

Omar Faisal exits.

SCENE SEVENTEEN

The hotel room.

SOHRAB: What did they say, Amir agha?

AMIR: They think there may be a way I can take you to America with me.

SOHRAB: They do? When can we go?

AMIR: Well, that's the thing. It might take a while.

SOHRAB: How long?

AMIR: I don't know. A while.

SOHRAB: I don't mind. I can wait. Will you take me to that red bridge?

AMIR: Absolutely.

SOHRAB: And we'll drive up the streets, the ones where all you see is the hood of the car and the sky?

AMIR: Every single one of them. But there is one thing, Sohrab.

SOHRAB: What?

AMIR: Well, it would really help if . . . if I could ask you to stay in a home for kids for a while.

SOHRAB: (*pause*) You mean an orphanage?

AMIR: It would only be for a little while.

SOHRAB: No, no, please.

AMIR: But, Sohrab, it wouldn't be for very long.

SOHRAB: You promised you'd never put me in one of those places.

AMIR: This is different. It would be here in Pakistan, not in Kabul.

SOHRAB: Please, no, Amir agha!

AMIR: I'd visit you all the time until we can get you out and—

SOHRAB: I don't want to go! They'll hurt me!

AMIR: No one is going to hurt you.

SOHRAB: Yes, they will! They always say they won't but they lie!

AMIR: It'll be all right.

SOHRAB: Please, no!

Sohrab hugs Amir in an act of desperation.

AMIR: You'll see.

SOHRAB: Promise you won't! Please promise you won't, Amir!

AMIR: (*yelling in frustration and pushing Sohrab away*) I can't promise that now, Sohrab! I just can't!

Pause.

SOHRAB: I'm so tired of it.

AMIR: Tired of what?

SOHRAB: Tired of everything. I want my old life back.

AMIR: I'm sorry.

SOHRAB: I'm going to take a bath.

Sohrab exits.

AMIR: While Sohrab was in the bathroom, I fell asleep.

Pause. Then a telephone rings.

Hello?

SORAYA: Amir?

AMIR: Hi.

SORAYA: How did it go at the embassy?

AMIR: Not good.

SORAYA: (*excited*) Well, my uncle made a few calls to his friends in the immigration service, and guess what? We can get Sohrab a humanitarian visa by next week!

AMIR: You're kidding. Next week?

SORAYA: Yeah, can you believe it?

AMIR: That's great!

SORAYA: He said the visa would be good for a year, plenty of time to apply for an adoption petition! It looks like it's really going to happen! The den upstairs can be his room and—

AMIR: Let me tell Sohrab! I'll call you right back, okay?

SORAYA: Okay, bye.

AMIR: Soraya?

SORAYA: Yeah . . .

AMIR: Ma dost et darom.

SORAYA: I love you, too.

Soraya exits.

AMIR: Sohrab! We're going to America! Do you hear me? We're going to California! (*To us.*) I pushed open the bathroom door!

Beat.

I saw bloody bathwater, an arm dangling over the side of the tub, and a blood-soaked razor on the toilet tank. And I started screaming. I was still screaming when the ambulance arrived. At the hospital, they put a white sheet over him and wheel him away.

Beat.

And I know what I have to do.

Amir gets down on his knees and assumes the position for prayer.

I haven't prayed in over fifteen years, so I say the few words I still remember: La illaha il Alla, Muhammad u rasul ullah. There is no God but Allah, and Muhammad is his messenger. La illaha il Alla, Muhammad u rasul ullah. La illaha il Alla, Muhammad u rasul ullah. La illaha il Alla, Muhammad u rasul ullah! LA ILLAHA IL ALLA, MUHAMMAD U RASUL ULLAH!

Beat.

I see now Baba was wrong. There is a God, always has been. I see Him here in the hospital, and I pray He forgives me. Forgive I lied, sinned, and betrayed all these years only to turn to Him now in my hour of need. My hands are stained with Hassan's blood! I pray God doesn't let them get stained with the blood of his son, too!

Amir continues to pray as the Pakistani Doctor enters.

(*repeating, softly*) Khoda koumakem koh. [*God help me.*] Khoda nejawtem betay. [*God save me.*]

PAKISTANI DOCTOR: Excuse me.

Amir scrambles to his feet.

PAKISTANI DOCTOR: Are you the boy's father?

AMIR: His uncle. How is he?

PAKISTANI DOCTOR: It was a very deep cut. He lost a great deal of blood. We transfused several units of red cells and twice had to revive him. If his heart hadn't been young and strong, we would have lost him. But he is alive.

AMIR: Oh, thank you, doctor. Thank you so much.

PAKISTANI DOCTOR: Children must be tended to, you know.

AMIR: Yes . . . yes, I know. I'm sorry.

PAKISTANI DOCTOR: Can I say something else to you?

AMIR: Sure.

PAKISTANI DOCTOR: The thing about you Afghans is that . . . well . . . you people are a little *reckless!* Take care of him.

Pakistani Doctor exits.

AMIR: Sohrab lived, but something died between him and me. He stopped talking. He was just blank, silent. It was like he had pushed a button and shut everything off.

SCENE EIGHTEEN

AMIR: And so it was that we arrived home on a warm day in August 2001. But while Sohrab was silent, the world was not. One Tuesday morning, the Twin Towers came crumbling down, and the world changed. America bombed Afghanistan and the Taliban scurried like rats. I'd go into a Starbucks and people would be talking about the cities of my childhood. And during all this, Sohrab didn't say a word.

A park in the San Francisco Bay Area. The sound of birds in the distance. Soraya, General Taheri, and Sohrab enter. Sohrab sits on the ground by himself.

Then, one Sunday afternoon, I took Sohrab, Soraya, and her father to a gathering of Afghans at a local park.

GENERAL TAHERI: So, Amir, are you going to tell me why you brought back that Hazara boy with you?

SORAYA: What kind of question is that!

GENERAL TAHERI: While you've been busy turning dens into children's bedrooms, my dear, I've had to deal with the community's perception of our family. People ask. They want to know why a mute Hazara boy is living with my daughter. What should I tell them?

SORAYA: Tell them it's none of—

AMIR: It's okay, Soraya. General Sahib is right. People do ask.

SORAYA: But, Amir, it's—

AMIR: It's all right.

Standing his ground and looking General Taheri in the eye.

> You see, General, my father slept with his servant's wife. She bore him a son named Hassan. Hassan is dead now. That boy is Hassan's son. My nephew. That's what you tell people when they ask. Oh, and one more thing. You will never again refer to him as "Hazara boy." His name is Sohrab.

Amir continues to stand his ground. General Taheri takes a breath, then exits, defeated. Soraya smiles at Amir. She exits after her father.

SORAYA: Padar jan . . .

AMIR: (*to us*) I walked into the field where a man was selling kites. I bought one and took it over to Sohrab.

Amir kneels next to Sohrab.

AMIR: (*to Sohrab*) Did I ever tell you your father was the best kite runner in all of Kabul? He always knew exactly where the kites would fall.

Sohrab doesn't respond.

> You want to help me fly this kite?

Sohrab still doesn't respond.

> Okay, looks like I'll have to fly it by myself.

Amir stands.

Last chance . . .

He embodies the following description.

AMIR: (*to us*) I took off running and let the spool roll in my hand.
Suddenly, I was twelve again and the old instincts came rushing
back.

Beat.

Then I saw we had company. Another kite was closing in on
ours. Hey, Sohrab, let's teach him a lesson. We'll let him get a
little closer. Come on, come to me. (*To us.*) The other kite was
inching closer, making its move, unaware of the trap I'd set for
it. (*To Sohrab.*) Watch this, Sohrab! I'll show you one of your father's favorite tricks. (*To us.*) I pulled hard and our kite plum-
meted! I could feel our string cutting his! Heard the snap! Then
the other kite was spinning out of control! (*To Sohrab.*) You see
that, Sohrab!?

Amir looks over at Sohrab, who is smiling slightly.

AMIR: (*to us*) A smile. Barely there. But there. (*To Sohrab.*) You want
me to run that kite for you?

Sohrab nods, no longer smiling.

For you, a thousand times over.

Amir hands Sohrab the spool.

AMIR: (*to us*) It was only a smile, a tiny thing. But I'll take it with
open arms. Because when spring comes, it melts the snow one
flake at a time, and maybe I just witnessed the first flake melt-
ing. Then I ran. A grown man running after a kite, but I didn't
care. I ran with the wind blowing in my face. I ran.

End of play.